Around the World in 45 Years

Charlie Brown's Anniversary Celebration

by Charles M. Schulz

Andrews and McMeel
A Universal Press Syndicate Company
Kansas City

 For information write Andrews and McMeel, a Universal Press Syndicate Company, 4520 Main Street, Kansas City, Missouri 64111.

ISBN: 0-8362-1766-7 (paperback)
0-8362-1772-1 (hardback)

Library of Congress Catalog Card number: 94-72371

00 01 BAM 10 9 8 7 6 5 4

Around the World in 45 Years

Foreword

by Lynn Johnston

It's eight years now since my husband, Rod, and I made our first visit to Sparky and Jeannie Schulz's home in Santa Rosa, California. It's a welcome place overlooking a lovely valley. We went for a long walk together, following a path through their property and, having worn only dress shoes, I had borrowed a pair of Sparky's sneakers with Kleenex stuffed into the toes! When we returned to the house for tea, it occurred to me that, not only had I been talking to a man I'd admired for years (and never expected to meet), but I had just walked a mile in his shoes!!

Over the years, we have shared many walks, had many talks, and it's these times I've treasured most. When I began my own comic strip in 1979, Sparky was one of the first cartoonists to call me and tell me I was doing fine. It was an expression of faith and friendship that pulled me together when I was plagued with doubts about my ability to turn out something worthwhile 365 days a year.

After all, we work with a powerful medium. Every day, our characters, who are extensions of ourselves, in a way, perform for millions of people worldwide! Our thoughts, our ideas, and our philosophies are expressed openly to an unseen audience whose response (if any) comes much later—and, by mail!

There is a great joy in being able to make someone think or laugh or identify with you from thousands of miles away. There is also great frustration when the inevitable criticism comes and hits like a punch to the jaw! (Criticism that comes despite your good intentions.)

One of the things we've talked about is "Success." Success in this business is defined by the syndicates in numbers—numbers of papers—numbers of readers—but, the real success for us is personal. Success is in producing an art form that comes from the heart, in working alone, in having the discipline required to feed the insatiable deadlines that come too fast, hungrily swallowing idea after idea. Ideas don't come easily—and often, don't come at all. Success is filling that space every day with work we are proud of. It's something we most definitely earn!

Interviewers love to ask, "Where do the ideas come from?" Well, nobody knows! All of us know the roller coaster that takes us racing to the top when the writing goes well and funny pictures appear—but, the plunge down into that well of anxiety when the page remains blank (sometimes for days!) can leave you green and exhausted and wishing life had dealt you a less-challenging hand!

If it all came too easily, I suppose the satisfaction in producing a really good gag wouldn't be so great! It's that rush of accomplishment that makes this job exciting—but, it's the downhill ride that keeps us sharp, in constant competition with ourselves—and keeps us humble!

So many times, I have imagined myself quitting this business. So many times, I have longed for a vacation from thought! These are the times when I compare myself to someone who has produced consistently for forty-five years a stream-of-consciousness called Peanuts and I say to myself, "If Sparky can do it—then so can I!"

We are a fragile lot. Most of us would not be able to survive without the reassuring presence of a telephone. The call that Sparky made to me in 1985 not only gave me strength and confidence, but showed me that a lifeline exists between cartoonists, connecting our studios from country to country, from coast to coast. We are a unique species. We are a community who, despite the ongoing competition for space in a declining number of newspapers, defends, supports, and encourages one another with sincerity and affection. We admire each other's achievements. We share and we commiserate—for, nobody understands a cartoonist like another cartoonist!

We are writers, artists, directors, performers, editors, and cameramen for a Lilliputian stage! Each of us struggles daily, trying to be the best we can be for ourselves and for our audience. Each of us sees potential in our characters to go beyond the confines of a tiny space on a printed page and, each of us measures our work against the yardsticks set for us by the masters of our craft.

This year, "For Better or For Worse" celebrates its fifteenth anniversary. I am now one of the "middle guard"! It's my turn to join those with experience in welcoming and reassuring the men and women who are new to the industry, bringing with them fresh, innovative ideas and diverse drawing styles. It will be my pleasure to extend the lifeline, to make the introductions, and to watch the new stars rise. Fifteen years! The time has gone by so fast!!

Last Christmas, Sparky and I wandered into a bookstore to buy a gift for his daughter. Only one of his books was on the shelf in the "Humor" section. "My books aren't number one anymore," he told me. "It's hard to step aside." I wasn't able to put my thoughts into words at the time. I'd like to do so now.

Dear Sparky:

When one has created a monument, it remains on this earth long after the craftsman has vanished. When one has left a legacy, it is divided and divided through generation after generation, the fragments becoming more valuable, more meaningful as the years go by. The cartoonists of tomorrow will inherit Peanuts as we have inherited the great works from our past. It isn't possible for you to "step aside"!

The swath that has been cut by this gently powerful collection of thoughts and images goes on indefinitely. Long after our pens are encased in plastic, artists and humorists will be following your footsteps—trying to catch up! I hope to be one of them.

As a friend and a colleague, I want to tell you that—I may have walked a mile in your shoes but—it will be a long, long time, if ever, before anyone will be able to fill them!

Happy forty-fifth Anniversary, Sparky! and here's to many more.

Love,

Around the World in Three Dimensions

by Connie Boucher

I've loved the Peanuts comic strip from the start. Its humor is ageless and so appealing. I'd always wanted to meet Charles "Sparky" Schulz. Then one day when I was sitting at the breakfast table reading the morning comics I had an idea that changed my life forever. I looked up at the calendar to see if it was my carpool day for the kids and suddenly I thought, "Peanuts calendar." Sparky and I both live in the San Francisco area so I called his office and told him I'd like to make a Peanuts calendar. I knew I was taking a chance calling him out of the blue but I figured it was worth a try. And it was! He liked the idea! I put a second mortgage on my house to pay for production costs and the following year my partner, Jim Young, and I introduced the Peanuts gang to the world of merchandising with the *1961 Peanuts Datebook*. It was a huge hit. Until this time character merchandising was virtually unknown. But with the appearance of Snoopy and the other Peanuts characters on a calendar the merchandising and licensing business was changed forever.

Since the very beginning, Sparky has worked closely with us to help make certain every piece of Peanuts merchandise is top quality. He makes sure that each product meets his high standards by getting personally involved in product development and maintaining a strict approval process. It's no secret that I've been more than a little frustrated with him at times for rejecting what I felt were good products, but upon reflection I understand and appreciate his high expectations. It's Sparky's personal involvement that has helped make Peanuts merchandise so popular.

Working with just a verbal business agreement, we began work on our second big Peanuts hit —*Happiness Is a Warm Puppy*. Based on one simple Peanuts comic strip, this little square-shaped book, designed by my partner while in the hospital, became the No. 1 bestseller of adult books in 1963, as well as a top-selling children's book. Schoolteachers adopted *Happiness Is a Warm Puppy* as a supplementary text in their classes. Sparky received *Happiness Is . . .* books created by schoolchildren for many years after. Now "Happiness Is . . . " phrases have come into everyday language—newspaper headlines, bumper stickers, billboards. It's amazing how, with just one delightful strip, Sparky created a best-selling book, a new catch phrase, and years of laughter.

The demand for Snoopy and his pals grew. Few people realize that the Peanuts characters helped popularize the sweatshirt fad by combining brightly colored sweatshirts with clever art and captions by Sparky. We struggled to get those shirts produced. We talked to dozens of banks before finding one who believed in financing this project. Factories were unable to provide the innovative colors we wanted so we mixed our own dyes. Regular apparel stores rejected the new concept so we wound up selling them in bookstores. Bookstores loved the shirts' witty captions—Charlie Brown saying "I Need All the Friends I Can Get"; Snoopy pondering "I Think I'm Allergic to Morning"; or Linus philosophizing "I Love Mankind, It's People I Can't Stand." All our hard work was worth the effort. Soon the market was flooded with imitations.

Until then most of us had only thought of Snoopy as a two-dimensional character. Charlie

Brown was the only one who knew the joy of hugging that lovable beagle every night before going to sleep. But all that changed in 1968 when we introduced a cuddly white plush Snoopy animal. When I first talked to store buyers they warned me that no practical mother would buy a white plush dog. But Sparky and I thought kids everywhere would love this huggable companion, so we persisted. Snoopy soon became a bedtime favorite. And when we added a line of clothes for Snoopy dolls, sales went off the charts.

It was hard to transform Snoopy from a flat comic strip character to three dimensions. While Sparky could visualize Snoopy's every curve, we made more than two dozen prototypes in an effort to get every detail perfect. We rejected prototype after prototype before we came up with a Snoopy plush good enough to show Sparky. However the minute we showed Sparky we knew we had the right Snoopy. Sparky's smile was instant approval!

By the early seventies there was no stopping Snoopy and his friends. Peanuts bedding soon became a winner with children and adults. When I first proposed the idea everyone thought I was crazy. No one believed children, much less adults, would want Snoopy printed on their sheets. But with Sparky's support, I pushed ahead. It wasn't easy, but before long sales of Peanuts bedding were in the millions.

This was just the beginning of what has become an international merchandising empire. Two generations of kids have a special place in their hearts for Peanuts and new fans are born everyday. We all have a little Snoopy, Charlie Brown, or Lucy in us and it's nice that we're able to indulge this with a Peanuts T-shirt, wristwatch, doll, or whatever. Sparky has created a true ageless classic. His perfect blend of simple art, amusing philosophies and insistence on top quality have made Snoopy and the Peanuts gang among the most popular merchandised characters in history. Thanks Sparky!

—Connie Boucher
Determined Productions

From St. Paul to Santa Rosa

by Charles M. Schulz

WHEN I WAS A CHILD, my hair was cut quite regularly by my dad in his barbershop. Sometimes, however, an important customer would come in before he was finished with me, and he would ask if I would sit on the bench while he took care of the customer. I was always terribly embarrassed having to sit on the bench with a half-finished haircut.

I had the very first *Famous Funnies* comic book that was ever published, but somehow it gradually disappeared. I know the cover was torn off by two arguing, visiting relatives. Comic books and Big Little books were an obsession with me, and I used to buy every one that came out until I was finally overwhelmed. Every now and then, my dad would ask me if I had any extra comic books that I didn't care about anymore that he could put in the barbershop for children to read while they were waiting to have their hair cut. It has since occurred to me that a lot of collector's items were trashed on that barbershop bench.

I doubt if we ever really get over the loss of our parents. My mother died a very cruel death from cancer when I was twenty years old and about to be drafted into World War II. I think of her often, and when I am thinking of my own children and their going to school and my own activities in school, I look back with great sadness upon something which in those days puzzled me a good deal.

Our school had a little monthly contest wherein the class that had the most parents attend one of the evening PTA meetings would be rewarded with a cake and ice cream interlude a few days later. I recall that our class won at least two or three times, but I always felt puzzled and I suppose somewhat guilty, because I knew that my mother had not attended any of these afternoon PTA sessions.

I am afraid my mother simply did not feel she was sophisticated enough to mingle with the other parents. This, of course, would have been completely untrue, for, although my mother went no further than the third grade, she certainly knew how to talk with other people. Perhaps she felt that she did not have the right type of clothes. I do not know.

I do know, however, that the fact that my dad owned his own business, a barbershop, made him almost a rarity in the neighborhood where I was growing up. Many of the fathers were actually unemployed. It would have been wonderful if someone could have explained to my mother that she need not have felt inadequate. I was always proud of both her and my dad, and look back upon these episodes with great sadness.

Little pencil sketches like this are used to develop ideas. Sometimes they work, and sometimes they don't.

Ever since I was very small, our family has always had at least one dog, starting with a Boston bull named Snooky who was hit by a taxicab one night when she was nine years old. I had prayed that she would survive, but she did not and it was a very sad time for me.

Our next dog was the dog named Spike after whom Snoopy was slightly patterned, mainly in his appearance and marking. Spike, however, was not really a beagle. But, of course, Snoopy was not a beagle when the strip first began, either. In fact, I think it took Snoopy almost the better part of ten years before he was labeled a beagle, simply because I think the word beagle is a good word.

I have always had a certain fondness for dogs, but also must admit that most of my life I have been a little bit afraid of them. I always approach dogs with much wariness because I am never quite sure what they are going to do.

With my own family of five children, we had many dogs. We had a couple of beagles. We had a St. Bernard who, unfortunately, died when she was only three, and a huge English sheepdog. We had several golden retrievers, and I am always amused by the fact that golden retrievers seem to be pretty much alike. They are wonderful dogs—very trustworthy—very loving, but pretty much all alike.

It was not until we had our last dog, Andy, that I developed a fanatical love for this funny little fuzzy dog. Up until then, I always just liked having the dogs, never really paying much attention to them.

Those of us who have been fortunate enough to have children know how much we worry about injuries though, of course, in the comic strip, people are always getting hit on the head with either a baseball or somebody like Lucy is pulling away the football so that poor Charlie Brown falls flat on his back when he tries to kick it. But strange and funny things do happen in real life.

When our son Craig was about nine years old, he had been left home with his brothers and sisters while my wife and I had gone off to Anderson, Indiana, for a rather dignified affair. The night before the big banquet, my wife decided that she would call home from our motel just to see how things were. My secretary answered the phone. My wife said, "How is everything at home?" And she said, "Oh, everything is fine, the ambulance just left."

For a sudden response, that's always been one of my favorites. Actually, what happened was Craig had gone off horseback riding in the woods with his older sister, and his horse had bounced him against a tree, breaking his leg, which meant that the next day we had to get into our car and start the long drive home. But that's always been one of my favorite punch lines.

In Santa Rosa, where I live, we have what is considered certainly one of the world's most beautiful ice arenas. We deal in all sorts of affairs. The figure skaters show up at 5:30 or 6:00 in the morning for their practicing. We have school programs where we bus in schoolchildren from around the city. They are given a half-hour lesson, and then are allowed to skate on their own for a half hour, and then they are bused back to whatever school they happen to come from.

We also have a full hockey program, not only for the younger children, but also for the older men. And in July, we usually host what is considered to be the finest senior hockey tournament in the world. We start at the age of forty, and last year, going in five-year age brackets, we actually broke the seventy barrier, so we had four teams composed of men over seventy. These players come from all over the world. We have had teams from Finland, and a regular entry from Japan. We've also had teams from Australia, Austria, and Switzerland.

Last year, we had 56 teams in the tournament, and we had 188 teams apply. Unfortunately, we can't accommodate that many entries, because the tournament can only run during one week and we can't get that many games in. We also have a roller blade show each year, and a roller blade camp across the street from the arena is run by my daughter, Jill. Two weeks before Christmas, we put on an ice show of which we are extremely proud. Former Ice Follies star Karen Kresge choreographs the show for me and she and I discuss it for several months before show time, trying to pick out some of our favorite songs and decide which direction the show is going to go.

Last year's show was responsible for a very strange story involving one of our favorite people, Judy Sladky. Judy and her husband were actually five-time national dance champions, so she is an extremely talented and accomplished skater and loves skating inside the Snoopy costume. Last year, the show had been running for over two weeks when Judy skated off the ice, and through the curtains, and through some unfortunate misstep broke the lower portion of one of her legs in two different places. She said that as soon as she put her foot down, she knew that she had broken her leg.

Now, she is lying on her back behind the curtain and the first thing she did was to say, "Tell Karen that I have broken my leg and somebody else is going to have to skate Snoopy." The people helping behind the curtain had taken the Snoopy head off the costume so Judy was lying on her back with the main body part of the costume still on, but the head off.

The ambulance came very quickly and the people, working gingerly, carried her out and placed her in the back of the ambulance. As they were heading across town toward the hospital, one of the attendants was on the phone to the people in the hospital, who asked the attendant, "Were you able to get a pulse down near her foot?" The attendant said, "Well, no, I can't because her paw is in the way." This must have been a strange response and must have confused the poor person in the hospital.

The ambulance finally arrived and they put her on a gurney but they discovered that with the huge Snoopy costume she could not fit on a normal-size gurney, so they had to get a maternity gurney. After she was wheeled into the hospital, they discovered something else. There were quite a few people in the emergency area and they couldn't take care of her right away, and they didn't quite know where to put her, so she was wheeled into the maternity ward.

Now, you can picture Judy inside the Snoopy costume with the huge stomach, lying flat on her back as people passed by, looking rather strangely at her, wondering what in the world this was. One nurse actually came into the room where Judy was lying, looked down at her and asked, "Are you sure you are in the right place?" And here, of course, is where we get the wonderful punch line, Judy being a very witty person. She turned to the nurse and said, "I don't know, I've never had a litter before."

I usually drive to our ice arena in the morning, where I have an English muffin and some grape jelly and a small cup of coffee. I love to read the morning paper at that time of day. As soon as I get out of the car, there are two dogs who realize that it is me. They live in a rented house on the corner, and as soon as I begin to walk toward them, they come running to the fence. One is a huge black Lab and the other is a very small dog—not quite a beagle—but very small and perky, and they immediately recognize me. I don't know if it's the car they recognize or if it's me.

Our Andy's veterinarian says that dogs observe the way you walk, so there is something about my appearance, even from a distance, that they recognize. They know I have a doggie biscuit for each of them. As I approach the fence, the huge Lab jumps high in the air, bounding with great delight at the prospect of this cookie. The other little dog sometimes barks, but most of the time comes close to the fence with his tail wagging furiously.

I always talk to them. I always say, "Hi, dogs, how are you today? I got the cookies." I walk up to the fence and the little dog moves down the fence a little bit so the big one won't get too near him, and I lean down and I say, "Here is a cookie for the little dog." And then the big dog looks up at me and I give him his doggie cookie. What is so pleasing is that as he puts the cookie in his mouth, he looks up at me, and our eyes meet. There is something about this that brings great joy to me.

I then walk across the sidewalk to the arena where I have the English muffin and the cup of coffee, knowing that these dogs have gotten my day off to a very nice start. It is a highly recommended program that I would suggest to anyone. Either get your own dog or make friends with some neighborhood dog. You will find it extremely gratifying.

We comic strip artists frequently feel that our profession is not regarded very highly on the artistic totem pole. When I first started drawing the Peanuts comic strip in 1950, I was given a very small space in which to work. Peanuts was sold as a space-saving comic strip, and each panel was drawn so it would fit neatly into one newspaper column. In other words, the strip could be printed horizontally, with each panel taking up one column, or it could be printed vertically, with the entire strip running down one column, or it could be printed two panels beneath the other two panels, forming a square. All of this was used as a sales gimmick for a feature in which, looking back, I believe indicated that the people at the syndicate really didn't have much confidence.

Not long after that, they came out with a couple of other features which were drawn to the full size that most comic strips were printed. This bothered me for a long time and, little by little, I have tried to increase the size of Peanuts in both the daily strip and the Sunday pages. Unfortunately, these sizes seem to be shrinking. But I came across a marvelous quote by S.J. Perelman: "To me, the muralist is not more valid than the miniature painter. In this very large country where size is all and where Thomas Wolfe outranks Robert Benchley, I am content to stitch away at my embroidery hoop." This was a most reassuring statement from that great humorist, and has helped to make me content to draw my tiny little comic strip every day.

Letters from readers can be most encouraging. One of my favorite letters of all time is the one relating to this strip, where someone who wrote to me said, "You have done your readers a distinct service by subtly suggesting that they look behind the scenes. I seriously doubt if Goliath had a mother worthy of the name. He swaggered and bullied in order to compensate for the lack of security which genuine mother love would have given him. My guess is that the only grief over Goliath's death was in the camp of the Philistines, mourning for themselves rather than for Goliath, for they no longer had him to fight their battles for them. Also, she probably wasn't much of a mother anyway."

I am always amazed at some of the things people say when they first discover what it is that I do for a living. "Oh," some of them exclaim, "are you still drawing the strip?" This is probably one of the most insulting things they could say. I am tempted to ask them, "Who do you think has been drawing it lately? Do you really think that the syndicate can go out and find just anyone to draw the strip?" But I suppose most people are under the impression that everyone who draws a comic strip has two or three people helping him or her.

Another question which continues to baffle me is, "Do you ever draw anything in your strip that has social meaning?" I have always felt that down through the years my strip has been filled with little tidbits of social meaning. I like to think that many of them are not obvious, but that I have had some important things to say.

In the August 24, 1992, edition of *Publishers Weekly*, I saw this quote: "This is a book with the intellectual depth of a cartoon strip." That's the kind of sentence that gets your day off to a bad start.

One evening recently, I was rereading a biography of James Thurber which I have next to my drawing board, and I came across the most wonderful quote. Thurber apparently had been accused of drawing cartoons which some critics felt did not have enough social criticism in them, and he replied, "Art does not rush to the barricades."

A wonderful lady named Selma Jacob from Kentucky asked me one day if she could use a line that I had written for the title of a book she was putting together. The line that I had written was, "Once you're over the hill, you pick up speed." She later told me she overheard a lady telling others, "Do you know that Selma Jacob wrote a book and the title of it was *Once You're Over the Hill, You Sure Slide Down Fast*."

I have done quite a few golf cartoons simply because I enjoy them. Golf lends itself to humor very much the same way that baseball does. One of my favorite stories concerns a friend of mine, Dr. Ward Wick, who died a couple of years ago and who was a true golf fanatic. I have never been able to work this into a cartoon, but it is certainly one of my favorite stories. Ward loved to practice golf and was standing out on the practice tee late one afternoon hitting a bucket of golf balls. An elderly gentleman, in this case, a Scotsman, stood watching him for some time. Finally, after hitting almost the whole bucket of balls, Ward turned to the gentleman and asked, "Well, what do you think?" And the gentleman replied, "Golf is not a violent game."

I am continually amazed when I discover there are people in the world who really do not have a sense of humor. One wonders why they even try to read comic strips and how much and how often they must be puzzled by what they read. The Sunday page shown here as an example shows Marcie saying to Peppermint Patty and the little boy, "Has the Lord spoken only through Moses?"

Now, I am not stupid enough not to know that this episode goes off in a different direction. But the quote that I used is certainly good for what I was drawing at that point. Nevertheless, I received letters from people who were under the impression that I had no idea what I was writing about.

How they could imagine I could even find such a quote without having a reasonable knowledge of the Old Testament is totally beyond me. One of the writers said, "I love the Bible, and biblical inaccuracy will not help your credibility." Another writer said, "If your Bible does not contain the entire chapter, we have included a copy of the entire story. Please read it carefully. It'll be extremely unfortunate if you allow your perversion of the meaning of the Word of God to stand. Please consider a public retraction." I have no idea how the writer thought I was going to make some kind of a retraction in a comic strip!

Another writer explained to me all about who Moses was and who his sister was and concluded by saying, "I hope this clarifies the subject for you. Put more questions in your comic strip if you like. I am always glad to instruct." Well, it is difficult for me to believe that these people could not see the humor in what I was trying to do and could not see that I must have some knowledge of what I was writing about.

Before I begin drawing any batch of daily strips or a Sunday page, I always check my calendar to see what the dates will be when the drawings will appear. Sometime in the early part of 1993, I was checking the calendar to see when the next Sunday page would appear. Much to my surprise, the next page would be June 6. Of course, it immediately occurred to me that that would be D-day.

Now, many cartoonists during the past few years have been devoting a complete page to one single drawing. A few are being given a half page, but most are allowed only a third page. I decided that a dramatic drawing for this June 6 D-day page would show Snoopy landing on one of the beaches at Normandy. It took me almost two days to run through all of the photographs I could find so that the drawing would have reasonable authenticity.

I was quite pleased and surprised at the response that this page got from readers. People from all over the country wrote to me thanking me for being the only one who remembered that this had been D-day.

Amazingly enough, when I was drawing the page it never occurred to me that the following year would be the fiftieth anniversary of the invasion and that there were going to be all sorts of commemorative exercises taking place around the country—but mostly in France. Now I had to begin to worry about what I would draw for the next June 6, fifty years after the invasion. I knew I had a fair amount of time to think about it, but of course, the months go by rapidly and as the time grew near, I knew I had to come up with something that would be quite original.

Somewhere I had read the reason Field Marshal Irwin Rommel was not at Normandy on June 6 was that his wife's birthday happened to be on that very day, and he had gone home to be with her. My research showed me that, as early as May 19, 1944, he had actually begun to think that he would probably have time to get away from his duties as the commander of the defense of the Coast of Normandy. His wife's name was Lucie-Maria. June 6 was to be Lucie's fiftieth birthday, and he had already ordered her a pair of handmade gray suede shoes, size 5½, in Paris. He estimated that he could leave the area of Normandy and be in Herrlingen on the morning of June 4. His weekly report had stressed that there was a fairly high degree of readiness on the part of the allies, but their past experience indicated that an invasion was not necessarily imminent, so he felt it was going to be all right to be gone.

This seemed to be the basis for what could be a good Sunday page involving Snoopy and his imagination and his activities as they might be the day before D-day, because this Sunday page was to come out on June 5, and, of course, the invasion was June 6.

I wanted to make sure that this research was correct and so I went through several different volumes to make sure that it was true that Rommel had gone home for his wife's birthday. I still had the problem, however, of trying to break it down into the panels of a Sunday page. How would Snoopy know this? Where would he be, and how could he communicate this knowledge (if he did have it) and how could the whole thing be presented as something serious, but have humor at the end?

The big problem, of course, is that Snoopy does not talk. We read his thoughts all of the time, but the kids who are with him cannot really hear those thoughts.

Snoopy had to be some kind of World War II GI and he would still have to be in England before the invasion took place. Somehow, the knowledge about Rommel going home could be Snoopy's, but how would he communicate this, and to whom would he be talking?

It occurred to me that I could put him in a little café with maybe someone like Peppermint Patty or Marcie, but I wanted to save Marcie to be a young girl Snoopy meets after he lands in France. Having Peppermint Patty be a young English lass seemed all right but, again, there was the matter of communication. Would she be the one who would tell him, or would he be the one who was trying to tell her? I couldn't make it work.

Actually, all of these thoughts were in my mind for almost a month before the day finally came when I knew I had to settle down and draw the page. One evening, while thinking about it, it occurred to me that if Linus were making a school report he could recite the background of what was happening and perhaps be telling the class how a certain young, unknown soldier happened to discover that Rommel was not going to be present at Normandy. This made it all quite simple, for I then could have Snoopy sitting by himself in an English pub, thinking about what was going to happen, and then rush off to phone General Eisenhower.

Of course, I still had the problem of Snoopy's inability to talk. I also had the problem of not really knowing what kind of telephones they had at that time in the London area. I knew that I wanted to draw one of the unique outdoor red booths that they had, but I didn't know what the telephones inside the booths looked like, and I couldn't seem to find any photographs that would show what they were.

As it happened, however, it worked out very well because Linus was able to say that the young hero, when he rushed off to call General Eisenhower, spoke in code. This is a pretty good example of how I sometimes need to overresearch an episode in order to make it finally work. What may appear to be a very simple cartoon may have a good deal more behind it than the reader realizes.

I have read of authors who have outlined the personality and the history of a character in a novel in order for them better to understand the character when they begin to write about him or her. While much of the information about this character may never be written, it helps the author better to understand what this character is like and how he or she may think or act under certain circumstances.

The same is true in a minor way with cartoon characters. I feel I know each one of these little personalities quite well and many of their attributes are known to me, even if in a vague way, which helps me to direct their actions when they are

D+2! THE WORLD FAMOUS G.I. DIGS A FOXHOLE..
HEY, CHARLIE BROWN, YOUR DOG IS DIGGING IN OUR BACKYARD!
SCHULZ
D+3..THE WORLD FAMOUS G.I. COMES ACROSS AN ABANDONED JEEP
HEY, CHUCK, WHY IS YOUR DOG SITTING OUT HERE IN A GROCERY CART?
SCHULZ
D+4! THE BRAVE INFANTRYMAN HURLS A GRENADE AT THE PILLBOX! THEN ANOTHER..AND ANOTHER!
WHY DO I HAVE THE FEELING SOMEONE IS THROWING ROCKS AT OUR FRONT DOOR?
SCHULZ
Dear Mom, Just a note to tell you I am well. They say we will be home by Christmas. I hope so.
SCHULZ

called upon to perform. If I happen to think of an idea, I can always turn to my repertory company and choose just the right character to act out this idea.

Many cartoons, of course, come from the personality of the characters themselves. The longer I live with the characters, the better I get to know them, and the more ideas they seem to provide.

If a character, by the very nature of the personality I have given him or her, provides me with ideas, then that character remains in the strip. If the character has attributes which are too distinct, such as the little boy, Pigpen, then he will not appear very often, because his appearance in the beginning of the cartoon will mislead the reader into thinking the idea is going to be something about the fact that he is dusty and dirty all of the time. In other words, Pigpen does not make a good straight man for any idea.

It is also absolutely essential that the readers build up their own ideas as to what the personalities are in these characters. This obviously means that I always have to be very careful to make sure that no one ever acts out of character.

Sometimes I wonder about Charlie Brown's attitude toward Lucy. Here she is, probably the most aggravating person he has ever known. He gets furious at her when she plays right field on his team. Sometimes, he feels he simply can't stand it. Each year, she somehow talks him into trying to kick the football, which she promises to hold, but she always pulls it away. He flies through the air, landing flat on his back, and then has to listen to some insane remark of hers to justify what she has just done.

Now, why in the world is he willing to pay money to receive some kind of five-cent psychiatric care? Our research shows he has visited her booth 119 times at a total cost of just over six dollars.

This, of course, does not mean that Lucy's life is perfect. She has her own problems. For some strange reason, she is totally fascinated by Schroeder, and I wonder why she is willing to hang around him, lean on his piano, and try to coax him into noticing her when it is obvious that he actually can't stand the sight of her. All he wants is to be left alone to play his piano; yet, there she is, leaning on the piano, saying these dumb things, trying to attract his attention. Why is she willing to do it, and why, I wonder, is her brother Linus willing to put up with her constant nagging?

I wonder why Linus, who is really a very bright little kid, has to cling to that blanket. And then I wonder why Snoopy is so anxious to grab this blanket from Linus. In the first place, I wonder what he's doing at Linus's house instead of remaining in his own backyard.

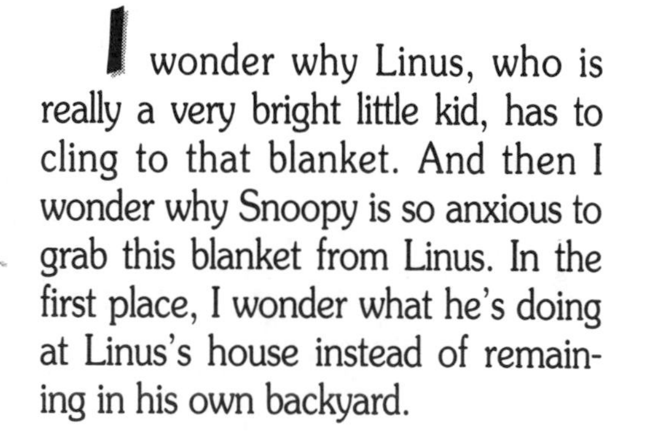

What is he doing over there? Linus just sits there, hanging onto the blanket, sucking his thumb, meditating with a wonderful sort of peace when Snoopy comes tearing by, grabs the blanket, and whirls him around in the air until they have a wild scramble. I wonder why Linus puts up with this. Why doesn't he tell Charlie Brown to keep his dog in his own backyard?

Then I wonder why Snoopy is willing most of the time to simply lie on the top of that doghouse. Why doesn't he roll off? I remember a veterinarian telling me once that when birds fall asleep sitting on a limb of a tree, their brain sends a message down to their claws telling the claws to stay clamped on the limb so the bird doesn't fall off and land on his head. So, I justify this by saying that perhaps it is the same way with Snoopy's ears. I think when he falls asleep, his ears clamp onto the top of the doghouse.

I still wonder why he lies up there. He doesn't look very comfortable. I suppose he has some form of claustrophobia that keeps him from going down into the doghouse. Or, maybe he just doesn't want to be trapped. A lot of dogs never go into doghouses because they don't want to be trapped. We bought a beautiful little doghouse for one of our dogs several years ago and he never even went near it—much less into it.

And then I wonder about Snoopy's extra adventures. It's perfectly all right that he has these daydreams where he thinks of himself as being the world-famous surgeon or the world-famous writer or, especially, the famous World War I flying ace. I think a dog who is leading kind of a boring existence has the right to escape into some kind of other world in order to help the days pass by. The only thing I wonder about is where in the world did he get the helmet and goggles?

I also wonder how he happens to know so much about France when he is walking through the countryside and stopping at little French cafés and flirting with the waitresses. How does he know exactly what to say and what to do and how does he know about all of those places that existed during World War I? I wonder where he did his research. I think it is something worth wondering about.

And then I wonder about those little birds that seem to trust Snoopy so faithfully. Woodstock, of course, is his closest friend. They have a strange relationship. I think they really like each other. They tease each other a lot, and Snoopy has a way of sometimes infuriating Woodstock. But like the other little birds, Woodstock follows him with complete trust as they go off on hikes, either up into the hills or through the woods, and seems to believe everything that Snoopy tells him.

I wonder where Snoopy got the idea that you can never be lost in the woods as long as you can see the moon? He says when you can see the moon, then you know you are facing west because the moon is always over Hollywood. I wonder where he got that idea? Why do the birds believe him?

And then I wonder about Snoopy's pathetic brother, Spike. Why does he think living out in the desert all by himself next to this huge cactus is the answer to all of life? I wonder what he eats. I wonder what he drinks, and I wonder why he is even safe out there in the desert. Sometimes I know he can hear coyotes howling in the distance at night and he must become very frightened, and I wonder why he is willing to put up with this.

And then I wonder why Marcie and Peppermint Patty are such good friends, and I wonder why Marcie continually calls Peppermint Patty "Sir," even though for a long while it aggravated Peppermint Patty no end, and she would continually say, "Stop calling me Sir." Marcie continues to do so, however, even though no one seems quite to know why.

They do like each other, however, even though they seem to be complete opposites. Marcie is a much better student and is not at all unwilling to help Peppermint Patty with tests when they have them in school and in other ways. But then, of course, once they leave the school building, Peppermint Patty seems to be the one who is more worldly-wise. Obviously, she is much more athletic, and I wonder why she is able to tolerate the complete ineptness of Marcie when it comes to playing baseball and football and the other things they do. Marcie seems to have no comprehension of these games and is one of the most naive athletes that ever existed.

I also wonder why Marcie seems to have to put up with some kind of pressure from home to be a good student. One day, she actually went over to Charlie Brown's house and fell asleep on the couch because she said she was simply under too much stress. What kind of parents does she have? I always wonder about that. We seem to have received some hints that they both are very active in their jobs and that her mother is very successful in whatever it is she does. But are they putting too much pressure on Marcie?

And what kind of home life does Peppermint Patty have? We have received some vague hints that Peppermint Patty does not have a mother and that her father travels a little bit, which means that Patty sometimes stays up quite late at night because she doesn't like being home alone, which is why she is sleepy in school the next day. But, we really don't know what happened to her mother. Was there a breakup in the marriage, or did her mother die? We don't know. I wonder if we will ever find out?

And, of course, I wonder about Charlie Brown's sister Sally. Now, it could very well be that Sally is one of the dumbest little kids we have ever known. She is almost as aggravating to poor Charlie Brown as is Lucy. And, yet, there is a certain awareness that she has. She seems to be relatively bright about some things, and I wonder where this sort of inconsistency comes from.

I suppose I wonder about all of these things when I look at the characters, and I wonder if this is really not the way most of us actually are. We all have our inconsistencies. We all have our weaknesses, and we all have suffered from unrequited love.

While putting together this book, Andy, the little dog pictured with me on the back cover, died. He had been an unbelievable joy to me, and as I write this I am deeply sorrowful. One Sunday in October of 1988 my wife, Jeannie, drove sixty miles to a fox terrier rescue kennel to pick up this eight-year-old scruffy little dog who had been found wandering on a nearby beach.

Jeannie apologized for his odd looks and mangy coat, but said she was afraid *not* to take him. She felt he was so ugly nobody else would ever want him. "Andy" was scratched into the inside of his leather collar as if a child had written it. Once Andy's hair grew, and we left it alone, he turned out to be soft, fluffy, and cuddly.

Andy brought some new truths into my life. He taught me the wonderful love that a person can have for a dog. He used to lie in my lap and sleep and he would always lie on the couch next to me in the evening. If I happened to be watching TV, he would always jump up onto this leather couch and sleep there the entire evening. Now and then, he might wake up and lean over and stretch his paw out and kind of bump my arm and ask me for the first of several doggie cookies.

Andy spawned a series of ideas of which I was very proud. One day I had Charlie Brown say to his teacher, "I have decided that I am probably never going to amount to very much. I am never going to be a very good student. I am never going to be an athlete. In fact, I guess I probably will not be much of a human being, so I have made a decision. I have decided that I am going to devote the rest of my life to making my dog happy." This came to me because it is something I used to say to my secretaries as I was leaving the studio in the late afternoon. I would go out the door and say, "Well, I am going home now. I'm going to devote the rest of the day to making my dog happy." And this is where ideas like this come from.

In the back cover photo Andy is wearing a small box that connected him to "the invisible fence," an underground wiring system that trains a dog to stay within a certain boundary. Andy apparently was a born wanderer, but he quickly learned to stay within the boundary. His funny ways endeared him to us, but as the years went quickly by, his hearing and his vision began to diminish. During his last six months he had great difficulty finding his way around the house and our driveway. He would go around in strange circles trying to find his way to our front door. Most of his days were spent sleeping.

On the night of March 2, 1994, he began to tremble and seemed not to want to get up. At 2:30 in the morning, Jeannie woke me, and said, "I think Andy is dying. We should take him to the emergency animal hospital." The veterinarian said he would not last the night, so we had to make the terrible decision to put him down. We had a sign nailed to a tree in our driveway that said, "Please drive slowly. Small dog does not see or hear well." When Andy died I hammered it loose and angrily chopped it into pieces.

The strip shown here was inspired by my love for little Andy. I shall never never forget him.

Jeannie and Charles Schulz with Andy.

To France

In Paris, December 21, 1989, French Minister of Culture Jack Lang awards Charles M. Schulz the medal signifying *Commandeur de l'Ordre des Arts et des Lettres*, "Commander of The Order of Arts and Letters."

To Italy

In Rome, October 15, 1992, in a private ceremony at the Palazzo Lancellotti, Italian Minister of Culture Margherita Boniver presented Charles M. Schulz the Award of Merit.

Around the World and Home Again

A Year of Peanuts

WHEN YOU DIE, ARE YOU EVER ALLOWED TO COME BACK?
ONLY IF YOU HAD YOUR HAND STAMPED..
SCHULZ

TELL ME, AS A WORLD FAMOUS SURGEON, ARE MOST OF YOUR PATIENTS ANIMALS OR HUMAN BEINGS?
BOTH, I GUESS..
I USED TO OPERATE ON FISH, BUT FISH NEVER HAVE ANY MONEY
SCHULZ

SLEEP WELL, OL' PAL..TOMORROW WILL BE A NEW DAY, AND WE NEVER KNOW WHAT EXCITEMENT LIES AHEAD..
ACTUALLY, I CAN'T TELL ONE DAY FROM THE OTHER..
SCHULZ

HOW ABOUT THIS, MARCIE? IT LOOKS LIKE SHE GAVE ME AN "A" IN EVERY SUBJECT...
YOU'RE RIGHT.. HER "D-MINUSES" DO LOOK LIKE "A'S"
SCHULZ

YOU KNOW WHAT I THINK, CHUCK? I THINK YOU GET BETTER GRADES IF YOU'RE CUTE..
I'LL BET MY TEACHER WOULD HAVE GIVEN ME ALL "A'S" IF I LOOKED LIKE THIS..
I LIKED YOU FINE THE OTHER WAY..
THANK YOU, CHUCK
BOY, THAT HURTS YOUR EYES..
SCHULZ

I SUPPOSE A LONG-DISTANCE RUNNER LIKE YOURSELF WATCHES WHAT HE EATS..
ABSOLUTELY
AFTER I'M DONE, I ALWAYS EAT A POWER DOUGHNUT..
SCHULZ

MY GRAMPA SAYS THOSE WERE THE GOOD DAYS..

WHAT DAYS?

HE DOESN'T KNOW WHAT DAYS, BUT HE'S SURE THOSE WERE THE GOOD DAYS..
SCHULZ

THAT WAS FUN!
STUPID DOG!
SCHULZ

I'LL JUST SIT HERE, AND LET YOU DIVIDE THE COOKIES BETWEEN US..
DOGS CAN'T COUNT
SCHULZ

I'M SORRY I'M LATE WITH YOUR SUPPER..I STOPPED TO ADMIRE THE SUNSET..
THERE WAS A GLOW IN THE SKY LIKE I'VE NEVER SEEN BEFORE..
I DON'T THINK THERE'S A WORD THAT DESCRIBES HOW IT CAN MAKE YOU FEEL...
HUNGRY!
SCHULZ

SO HERE I AM RIDING ON THE BACK OF MY MOM'S BICYCLE..
THIS SHOULD BE A GOOD TRIP IF SHE STEERS STRAIGHT...
..AND IF OUR FRONT WHEEL DOESN'T GO DOWN THAT..
..GRATE!
SCHULZ

ALL RIGHT, TROOPS..BEFORE YOU GO TO SLEEP, I WANT TO HEAR SOME BEDTIME PRAYERS..
I DIDN'T KNOW THEY HAD THEOLOGICAL DIFFERENCES..
SCHULZ

CHOMP
CHOMP
NO, NOT AT ALL..
NO, MA'AM..I CAN'T SEE THE QUESTION ON THE BLACKBOARD
BUT DON'T DESPAIR, MA'AM..I'M EATING CARROT CAKE!
YES, MA'AM.. A LITTLE MID-MORNING SNACK..
CARROTS ARE GOOD FOR YOUR EYES.. YOU KNEW THAT, DIDN'T YOU, MA'AM?
THERE! THAT WAS GREAT!
OKAY, NOW LET'S TAKE ANOTHER LOOK AT THAT QUESTION ON THE BLACKBOARD...
I CAN SEE IT! THE CARROT CAKE DID ITS JOB!
YES, MA'AM, I CAN SEE THE QUESTION, BUT I STILL DON'T KNOW THE ANSWER..
DON'T SIGH, MA'AM..EATING CARROT CAKE IN THE MORNING MAKES YOU WEIRD..
SCHULZ

SOMETIMES, CHUCK, I WONDER IF YOU EVER REALIZE JUST HOW EMBARRASSING THIS CAN BE..

BONK
LUCY, YOU'RE THE WORST PLAYER IN THE HISTORY OF THE GAME!
YOU CAN'T PROVE THAT! YOU SHOULD NEVER SAY THINGS THAT YOU CAN'T PROVE!
IN ALL PROBABILITY, YOU ARE THE WORST PLAYER IN THE HISTORY OF THE GAME!
I CAN ACCEPT THAT..
SCHULZ

DID YOU KNOW THAT BLACKBEARD, THE PIRATE, BURIED ALL HIS GOLD HERE IN THE DESERT?
AND THAT BLACKBEARD ONCE SPENT THE NIGHT IN A MOTEL IN NEEDLES? THAT'S WHAT SOMEONE TOLD ME..
YOU DON'T BELIEVE ANYTHING, DO YOU?
SCHULZ

Dear Pen Pal, How have you been?
WHY DO YOU HAVE A PEN PAL?
TO LEARN ABOUT OTHER CULTURES... HE TELLS ME ABOUT HIMSELF, AND I TELL HIM ABOUT ME..
WHY WOULD ANYONE WANT TO HEAR ABOUT YOU?
Some days I feel like I'm writing uphill.
SCHULZ

HERE, BOY!
"BOY"?
GET IT!
GET IT, BOY! GET THE BALL!
THAT'S THE WAY! GOOD DOG!
GET IT, PAL!
THAT'S THE WAY! BRING IT HERE!
GET IT, BOY! GET THE STICK!
THATTA BOY! BRING IT BACK!
WHAT DID YOU DO FOR YOUR DAD FOR FATHER'S DAY, CHARLIE BROWN?
I LET HIM PLAY WITH MY DOG..
SCHULZ

HEY, KID.. REMEMBER ME? I'M ROY HOBBS' GREAT-GRANDDAUGHTER
I KNOW.. I'M VERY IMPRESSED
THE LAST TIME WE PLAYED, YOU HIT A HOME RUN OFF ME, AND RUINED MY LIFE!
I WAS JUST LUCKY
I SUPPOSE YOU THINK YOU'RE GONNA DO IT AGAIN..
WHAT'RE YOU TRYIN' TO DO NEXT, RUIN MY AFTERLIFE?
SCHULZ

YOU'RE UP NEXT, CHARLIE BROWN.. YOU CAN HIT THIS PITCHER! THE LAST TIME YOU FACED HER, YOU HIT A HOME RUN!
YOU CAN DO IT! YOU'RE THE HERO TYPE!
OR THE GOAT TYPE..
SCHULZ

THAT ROUND-HEADED KID IS UP NEXT, ISN'T HE?
SO WHAT? HE WAS JUST LUCKY THE LAST TIME WE PLAYED...
YOU'RE ROY HOBBS' GREAT-GRANDDAUGHTER, AREN'T YOU? WELL, SHOW 'IM WHO YOU ARE!
THROW IT IN HERE, ROYANNE!
ROYANNE?
SCHULZ

STRIKE ONE!
C'MON, CHARLIE BROWN! SHE'S NO PITCHER! SHE'S ONLY A GIRL!
ONLY A GIRL?!
WELL, I'M ONLY YOUR SISTER, YOU BLOCKHEAD!!

HEY, I THOUGHT I FELT A DROP OF RAIN..
I DID! IT'S RAINING!
STRIKE TWO!
HA! YOU'RE DOOMED, KID! YOU'RE GONNA STRIKE OUT!!
NO, I'M GONNA DROWN..

TWO STRIKES ON THAT ROUND-HEADED KID, AND IT STARTS RAINING!
MAYBE IT'LL STOP SOON..
YOU CAN GET A HIT, CHARLIE BROWN..DON'T LET THAT GIRL STRIKE YOU OUT!
SHE THROWS PRETTY HARD..
I'M A HOUSE DOG.. HOUSE DOGS AREN'T SUPPOSED TO GET WET

OKAY, TEAM.. WE'RE UP TO BAT!
SO I'VE BEEN WONDERING..
WHICH IS MORE IMPORTANT? WHICH IS THE GREATER ACCOMPLISHMENT?
WHICH WOULD YOU RATHER DO.. WRITE "WAR AND PEACE" LIKE LEO TOLSTOY...
..OR HIT SIXTY-ONE HOME RUNS LIKE ROGER MARIS?
STRIKE THREE!
I PROBABLY WON'T WRITE "WAR AND PEACE" EITHER..
SCHULZ

OKAY, KID, IT'S STOPPED RAINING, AND YOU GOT TWO STRIKES AGAINST YOU!
TIME OUT! ONE OF MY PLAYERS WANTS TO TALK TO ME...
THEY'RE HAVING A CONFERENCE, AREN'T THEY? THEY'RE PLANNING SOME CLEVER STRATEGY.. I JUST FEEL IT...
NO, LAST NIGHT YOU HAD YOUR SUPPER IN THE RED DISH AND WATER IN THE YELLOW DISH..
SCHULZ

CRACK!
HE HIT IT! CHARLIE BROWN HIT IT! THE BALL IS GOING TO THE FENCE! RUN, CHARLIE BROWN! RUN!
OH, NO! THE WORLD IS COMING TO AN END! I ALWAYS KNEW IT WOULD END THIS WAY!
SCHULZ

CHARLIE BROWN IS ROUNDING FIRST! HE'S ROUNDING SECOND! HE'S ROUNDING THIRD...
BUT ROY HOBBS' GREAT-GRANDDAUGHTER HAS THE BALL!! SHE'S BLOCKING THE PLATE!!!
SCHULZ

SLIDE, CHARLIE BROWN, SLIDE!!
SCHULZ

YOU DID IT, CHARLIE BROWN! YOU HIT ANOTHER HOME RUN, AND WE WON THE GAME!
YOU MEAN I WAS SAFE?
I'M ROY HOBBS' GREAT-GRANDDAUGHTER.. WHERE AM I? WHAT HAPPENED?
YOU WERE BLOCKING THE PLATE, SWEETIE.. HERE, I COULD ONLY FIND ONE SHOE..
SCHULZ

WELL, YOU DID IT AGAIN, DIDN'T YOU? YOU HIT ANOTHER HOME RUN, AND RUINED MY LIFE!
I WAS LUCKY
YOU ALMOST KILLED ME WHEN YOU SLID INTO HOME..
YOU WERE BLOCKING THE PLATE, SWEETIE..
I STILL CAN'T FIND MY OTHER SHOE...
I'M SORRY
I HATE GOING THE REST OF MY LIFE WEARING ONLY ONE SHOE
SCHULZ

YAWN
Z
Z
Z
Z
Z
Z
Z
Z
Z
Z
SCHULZ

THIS WOULD BE A MUCH BETTER WORLD IF DOGS COULD FLY, TOO..
IMAGINE A WARM SUMMER NIGHT...
AND OVERHEAD, A SKY FILLED WITH DOGS BARKING
SCHULZ

YOU KNOW HOW EVERYONE LIKES TO SEE GEESE FLYING ACROSS THE FACE OF A FULL MOON?
IF DOGS COULD FLY, WOULDN'T IT BE NEAT TO LOOK UP AND SEE A SAINT BERNARD FLYING ACROSS THE FACE OF THE MOON?
WELL, MAYBE NOT..
SCHULZ

ARE YOU AWAKE?
WHO WANTS TO KNOW?
I'M YOUR BROTHER... REMEMBER ME?
DO YOU HAVE ANY IDENTIFICATION?
SCHULZ

YES, I AGREE.. IT TAKES COURAGE TO SAIL IN UNCHARTED WATERS..

I'M NOT SURE I WANT TO GO TO CAMP..
WELL, YOU'D BETTER MAKE UP YOUR MIND... THE BUS LEAVES IN FIVE MINUTES!
I'LL BE THERE IN SIX MINUTES..

NO, SIR.. MY SISTER WON'T BE COMING TO CAMP THIS YEAR.. SHE MISSED THE BUS... BUT I'M HERE!
YES, SIR.. A YEAR AGO.. LAST PLACE IN THE SACK RACE.. UH HUH.. THAT WAS ME..
NO, I UNDERSTAND... YOU HAVE A LOT OF CAMPERS COME THROUGH HERE..
SCHULZ

"'AND I WISH YOU WOULDN'T KEEP APPEARING AND VANISHING,' SAID ALICE"
"'YOU MAKE ONE QUITE GIDDY'"
"'ALL RIGHT,' SAID THE CAT; AND THIS TIME IT VANISHED SLOWLY, ENDING WITH THE GRIN..'
I CAN DO THAT..
SCHULZ
READ SOMETHING ELSE...QUICK!

CALLING HOME, CHARLIE BROWN?
I THOUGHT I'D LET EVERYONE KNOW THAT I GOT HERE TO CAMP SAFELY..
"THANK YOU FOR CALLING THE BROWN RESIDENCE.. IF YOU KNOW THE FOUR DIGIT EXTENSION OF THE PARTY YOU ARE TRYING TO REACH, YOU MAY DIAL IT NOW.. IF YOU ARE CALLING YOUR SISTER, PRESS THREE.. IF YOU HAVE A ROTARY DIAL TELEPHONE, PLEASE HOLD FOR THE NEXT AVAILABLE PERSON..."
SCHULZ

HELLO? OH, IS THIS YOU, BIG BROTHER?
YOU'RE AT CAMP, AND I'M NOT! HA HA HA HA HA!!
NEVER CALL HOME!
SCHULZ

HI! MY NAME IS ETHAN.. I JUST GOT BACK FROM "CRAFTS"
WE'VE BEEN LEARNING HOW TO MAKE BOWS AND ARROWS LIKE THE INDIANS..
THIS IS THE ARROW I MADE..
THAT'S AN INDIAN ARROW?
SURE, WITHOUT IT, THEY WOULDN'T KNOW WHICH WAY THEY WERE GOING..
SCHULZ

WHAT DO YOU WANT TO BE WHEN YOU GROW UP, ETHAN?
A NEWSPAPER COLUMNIST..
I HAVE VERY STRONG OPINIONS ABOUT EVERYTHING
THAT'S A STUPID LOOKING SHIRT YOU'RE WEARING..
SCHULZ

HI, SALLY.. I'M COMING HOME THIS AFTERNOON...
HAS MY DOG MISSED ME?
OH, YES..HE'S BEEN WAITING FOR YOU...
WELCOME HOME, ROUND-HEADED KID!
SCHULZ

BAM! BAM!
ARE YOU UPSET, LITTLE FRIEND? HAVE YOU BEEN LYING AWAKE WORRYING? WELL, DON'T WORRY.. I'M HERE
I'M HERE TO GIVE YOU REASSURANCE.. EVERYTHING IS ALL RIGHT...
THE FLOOD WATERS WILL RECEDE.. THE FAMINE WILL END.. THE SUN WILL SHINE TOMORROW...
AND I WILL ALWAYS BE HERE TO TAKE CARE OF YOU!
BE REASSURED!
WHO REASSURES THE REASSURER?
SCHULZ

I KNOW IT'S HOT, MEN, BUT LET'S KEEP GOING..
NOT TOO FAR AHEAD IS AN OASIS WHERE THERE'LL BE LOTS OF WATER...
SCHULZ

IT IS SAID THAT WHEN DOGS DRINK FROM THE RIVER NILE, THEY DO IT WHILE RUNNING SO AS NOT TO BE SEIZED BY CROCODILES..
I FEEL RIDICULOUS
SCHULZ

JUST SPIT THEM OUT..
?
THOSE ARE BUTTONS..THEY KEEP THE WATERMELON FROM FALLING APART..
HE NEVER BELIEVES ANYTHING I TELL HIM
SCHULZ

FALLING ROCK
FALLING THINGS
SCHULZ

SO HERE I AM LEFT TO GUARD THE CAR WHILE THE FAMILY GOES SHOPPING..
ANYONE WHO COMES NEAR THIS VEHICLE WILL MEET A SNARLING TORNADO!
ON THE OTHER HAND, FOR TWO COOKIES THEY CAN HAVE THE CAR..
SCHULZ

SCHULZ

THIS IS KIND OF INTERESTING
" SOMETIMES WHEN A DOG IS ABOUT TO GO TO SLEEP, IT WILL TURN AROUND IN A CIRCLE BEFORE LYING DOWN.."
" THIS HABIT GOES BACK TO THE DOG'S WILD ANCESTORS WHO STAMPED DOWN THE GRASS TO FORM A NESTLIKE BED.."
WHAT DOES IT SAY ABOUT WAKING UP?
SCHULZ

Z
YOU KNOW WHAT'S WRONG WITH YOUR STORY? IT'S UNBELIEVABLY BORING!
A PERSON COULD FALL ASLEEP READING IT..
I FELL ASLEEP WRITING IT!
SCHULZ

I THINK YOU TAKE THIS GAME TOO SERIOUSLY, CHARLIE BROWN...
YOU PUT TOO MUCH STRESS ON YOURSELF..
YOU'RE PROBABLY RIGHT, LUCY.. THANKS FOR REMINDING ME..
TRY TO GET THE BALL OVER THE PLATE! YOU THINK WE'RE OUT HERE FOR THE FUN OF IT?!
SCHULZ

He was tough. He was mean.
They called him "Macho Beagle."
He carried his own felt pen.
SCHULZ

OKAY, SHOOT!
YOU DIDN'T SAY, "NICE TRY"
SCHULZ

GUESS WHAT, MARCIE.. I'VE BEEN DOING A LITTLE SUMMER READING..
MAYBE YOU CAN HELP ME.. WHY DID VANNA WHITE TAKE THE CARAMELED APPLE FROM THE WITCH?
"SNOW" WHITE, SIR.. AND IT WAS A PLAIN APPLE..
PRETTY PROFOUND STORY, HUH, MARCIE?
SCHULZ

MMMM!
BEAUTIFUL!
?
NO, I DON'T THINK SO..
?
OKAY, TAKE A LOOK IF YOU WANT TO..
I KNEW YOU WOULDN'T BE ABLE TO SEE HOW THEY GET THE JELLY INSIDE THE DOUGHNUT..
SCHULZ

DO YOU THINK IT'S POSSIBLE TO RIDE CLEAR ACROSS THE LAKE ON A BEACH BALL?
I DOUBT IT, WHY?
I WAS JUST WONDERING..
SCHULZ

DEAR GRANDMA, I AM DICTATING THIS LETTER TO MY SISTER SALLY WHO IS STUDYING SHORTHAND...
MAYBE YOU'D BETTER JUST CALL HER ON THE PHONE..
SCHULZ

SOMETIMES I LIE AWAKE AT NIGHT, AND I ASK MYSELF, "IS THIS ALL THERE IS?"
THEN I HEAR A VOICE THAT SAYS..
"WHAT KIND OF A QUESTION IS THAT?"
SCHULZ

IF YOU PAID SEVENTEEN DOLLARS FOR A MAILBOX AND YOU ONLY GOT ONE LOVE LETTER, IT WOULD STILL BE WORTH IT...
ON THE OTHER HAND, IF YOU NEVER EVER GET EVEN ONE LOVE LETTER, THEN YOU SHOULD GET YOUR SEVENTEEN DOLLARS BACK...
I'D LIKE TO SPEAK TO THE MANAGER, PLEASE..
SCHULZ

DID YOU KNOW OUR NAME IS IN THE PHONE BOOK?
SEE? THERE'S OUR NAME, OUR ADDRESS AND OUR PHONE NUMBER...
YOU NEVER TOLD ME WE WERE FAMOUS..
SCHULZ

IF OUR NAME IS IN THE PHONE BOOK, WHY ISN'T OUR NAME IN THE "OLD TESTAMENT"?
TRY GENESIS 30:32
"..AND ALL THE BROWN CATTLE AMONG THE SHEEP"
WOW!
SCHULZ

TIME OUT!
LISTEN TO ME, CHARLIE BROWN..
I THINK YOU SHOULD THROW NOTHING BUT FASTBALLS TO THIS NEXT GUY...
AND WATCH THE KID ON SECOND.. HE'S BEEN TAKING A BIG LEAD...
ANYTHING ELSE?
I THINK IT BROKE BEETHOVEN'S HEART WHEN GIULIETTA GUICCIARDI MARRIED COUNT VON GALLENBERG..
CATCHERS HAVE A LOT ON THEIR MINDS..
SCHULZ

YOU ARE MY YOUNGER BROTHER AND I AM YOUR OLDER SISTER, AND THAT'S THE WAY IT'S GOING TO BE ALL THE DAYS OF YOUR LIFE..
..AND DON'T TELL ME YOU NEVER THINK ABOUT IT..
SCHULZ

THE SUN IS IN YOUR EYES?
WELL, PUT ON SOME SUNGLASSES, OR WEAR A HAT OR SIT UNDER AN UMBRELLA..
..OR DO ALL THREE..
SCHULZ

YES, MA'AM..DO YOU HAVE ANY BOOKS HERE IN YOUR LIBRARY WHERE A DOG TAKES OVER THE WHOLE WORLD?
SCHULZ
WELL, I THINK NOW YOU'VE GOT ONE..

SCHOOL STARTS IN FOUR WEEKS!!
DETAILS AT ELEVEN..

YES, SIR.. WE'D LIKE TO BUY SOME SCHOOL SUPPLIES
THINGS LIKE PAPER AND PENCILS..
AND LOTS OF ERASERS..

YES, SIR.. YOU WANT TO KNOW WHY WE'RE BUYING OUR SCHOOL SUPPLIES SO EARLY?
TELL HIM WE'RE TRYING TO CREATE THE ILLUSION THAT WE'RE ANXIOUS TO BECOME EDUCATED..
WE JUST LIKE TO BE PREPARED
MY ANSWER WAS BETTER

WHY CAN'T I HAVE A NORMAL DOG LIKE EVERYONE ELSE?
SCHULZ

NOW, GET OUT THERE IN RIGHT FIELD, AND CONCENTRATE!
THINK ABOUT WHAT YOU'RE DOING..
KEEP YOUR MIND ON THE GAME..
KEEP YOUR HEAD OUT OF THE CLOUDS..
SCHULZ

ROYANNE! WHAT A SURPRISE!
I NEED TO TALK TO YOU, CHARLES..DO YOU HAVE TIME TO GO GET A CHOCOLATE SUNDAE?
OKAY, ROYANNE, WHAT'S UP?
DO YOU LIKE ME, CHARLES?
OH, GOOD GRIEF!
SCHULZ

I HAVE TO TELL YOU SOMETHING, CHARLES.. BUT FIRST, I WANT TO KNOW IF YOU LIKE ME...
WELL, SURE, I LIKE YOU, ROYANNE.. BUT I DON'T REALLY KNOW YOU..I MEAN, OUR TEAM PLAYED YOUR TEAM A COUPLE OF TIMES..
AND, OF COURSE, I HIT THOSE TWO HOME RUNS, AND..
THAT'S WHAT I HAVE TO CONFESS, CHARLES..I COULD HAVE STRUCK YOU OUT IF I HAD WANTED TO!
SCHULZ

YOU LET ME HIT THOSE HOME RUNS?!
I HAD TO, CHARLES..YOU LOOKED CUTE STANDING THERE AT THE PLATE..
I DIDN'T WANT TO LOOK CUTE!!
HOW ABOUT PATHETIC?
I CAN'T STAND IT!
SCHULZ

WHY DID YOU TELL ME YOU LET ME HIT THOSE HOME RUNS? I LIKED BEING A HERO..
I'M ROY HOBBS' GREAT-GRANDDAUGHTER.. I HAVE A REPUTATION
ROY HOBBS WAS A FICTIONAL CHARACTER
WHAT?!
DIDN'T YOU KNOW THAT?
MY LIFE IS RUINED..
WHEN YOUR LIFE HAS BEEN RUINED, YOU SHOULD LIE UNDER A TREE ALL AFTERNOON..
SCHULZ

SHE ASKED YOU TO GO OUT FOR A CHOCOLATE SUNDAE?
UH HUH.. AND THEN SHE CONFESSED THAT SHE HAD LET ME HIT THOSE HOME RUNS! I WAS CRUSHED!
I WAS HUMILIATED!
AND THEN SHE LET ME PAY FOR THE CHOCOLATE SUNDAES!
SCHULZ

I THINK THAT'S HER HOUSE THERE..
HI, CHUCK! THANKS FOR BRINGING YOUR DOG OVER..
MY DAD AND I ARE GOING TO BE GONE OVERNIGHT SO WE NEED A WATCHDOG TO GUARD THE HOUSE..
NOW, AROUND HERE IS THE BACKDOOR...
AND THIS IS THE ENTRANCE TO THE GARAGE..IF ANYONE COMES AROUND, HE SHOULD BARK LIKE MAD!
IT'LL PROBABLY BE BEST IF HE JUST STANDS GUARD HERE AT THE FRONT OF THE HOUSE, AND...
Z
Z
YOU SURE KNOW HOW TO GET OUT OF THINGS, DON'T YOU?
SCHULZ

HORSES ARE RELATIVELY EASY TO TRAIN..MULES ARE EASIER TO TRAIN THAN DONKEYS..IT TAKES PATIENCE TO TRAIN A DONKEY...A MULE IS ONE-HALF DONKEY AND ONE-HALF HORSE..
DON'T ALWAYS FEEL IT'S NECESSARY TO MAKE CONVERSATION, MARCIE..
SCHULZ

MISS DAVIS IS GOING TO BE SURPRISED WHEN SHE GETS THIS BOOK REPORT..
MISS DAVIS QUIT TEACHING TWO YEARS AGO..SHE GOT MARRIED, AND HAS A NEW BABY
MAYBE I COULD ATTACH A "CONGRATULATIONS" CARD TO THE REPORT..
SCHULZ

YOU KNOW WHAT WE SHOULD DO, MARCIE? WE SHOULD SIGN UP FOR RIDING LESSONS..
ON HORSES?
THERE AREN'T ANY ZEBRAS AROUND HERE, MARCIE..
SCHULZ

YOU'RE LATE.. WE'VE ALREADY STARTED EATING
THERE WAS HEAVY FIGHTING OVER ST. MIHIEL..
LINUS IS HAVING DINNER WITH US TONIGHT
WHY IS HE LOOKING AT ME SO FUNNY?
I'M NOT USED TO EATING WITH THE ENLISTED MEN
SCHULZ

IF YOU'RE GOING TO BE FLYING OVER PARIS, COULD I HITCH A RIDE?
IT'S AGAINST REGULATIONS, BUT I SUPPOSE WE CAN DO IT..
IS IT VERY FAR?
NO, THERE'S PARIS NOW..
HAVE A GOOD TIME!
SCHULZ

HEY, CHUCK..YOUR CRAZY DOG ALMOST KILLED ME!
POOR GIRL..WE WERE FLYING OVER PARIS AND SHE FELL OUT OF THE PLANE..
FORTUNATELY, WE WERE FLYING VERY LOW
YOU SHOULD DO SOMETHING ABOUT THAT DOG, CHUCK..
CIVILIANS SHOULDN'T BE ALLOWED ON THE AËRODROME..
SCHULZ

"'WHAT A CURIOUS FEELING,' SAID ALICE"
"SHE WAS NOW ONLY TEN INCHES HIGH.."
"NOW SHE WAS MORE THAN NINE FEET HIGH..."
"'HOW CAN I HAVE DONE THIS?' SHE THOUGHT."
"'I MUST BE GETTING SMALL AGAIN'.."
RIGHT
SCHULZ

TOO BIG FOR YOU? ALL RIGHT, BRING YOUR OWN BALL..
WHAT HAPPENS IF I SWALLOW IT?
SCHULZ

WHEE!
IT'S HARD TO EXPLAIN WHY BALLOONS ARE SO MUCH FUN
SCHULZ

HI! I GUESS YOU KNOW THAT SCHOOL STARTS NEXT WEEK..
BEFORE YOU KNOW IT, THOUSANDS OF SCREAMING KIDS WILL BE RUNNING THROUGH YOUR HALLS!
JUST THINKING ABOUT IT GIVES ME ROOM-ACHE!
SCHULZ

SCHOOL STARTS TOMORROW!!
WOULD YOU RECOGNIZE THE PRINCIPAL IF YOU MET HIM ON THE STREET ?! BE READY! BE READY!
SCHULZ

CLUMP CLOMP CLUMP CLUMP
HEY! YOU GOT SHOES!
THEY LOOK GREAT... YOU GOT SHOES JUST LIKE MICKEY MOUSE!
BUT LET ME ASK YOU SOMETHING...
WHAT DO YOU THINK OTHER BIRDS ARE GOING TO SAY? WHAT IF THEY TEASE YOU?
WHAT IF THEY SAY STUPID THINGS TO YOU LIKE, "DOES YOUR MOTHER WEAR ARMY BOOTS?"
WHICH LEADS ME TO ASK YOU SOMETHING ELSE..
DOES YOUR MOTHER WEAR ARMY BOOTS?
HAHAHA
THUMP!
I WONDER IF MICKEY'S MOM WORE ARMY BOOTS..
SCHULZ

AFTER I GRADUATE FROM SCHOOL, WILL I BE A BETTER PERSON?
PROBABLY.. A GOOD EDUCATION IS VERY IMPORTANT
THAT'S RIGHT.. LEARNING ALWAYS MAKES YOU A BETTER PERSON..
UNLESS YOU DON'T HAVE A DOG..
SCHULZ

Z
YES, MA'AM.. I'M AWAKE!
DO I HAVE ANYTHING TO TELL THE CLASS? YES, MA'AM..
THERE'S A SPIDER ON THE CEILING..
SCHULZ

HEY, MARCIE, WE DON'T HAVE ANY HOMEWORK TONIGHT, DO WE? WE **DO**?!
PAGE SIXTEEN? PAGE SIXTEEN OF WHAT?
A BOOK? WHAT BOOK?
DON'T HANG UP, MARCIE..
SCHULZ

SORRY, MA'AM..I WASN'T LISTENING..I WAS THINKING ABOUT MY DOG...
HE ALWAYS WAITS FOR ME TO COME HOME.. NO, HE DOESN'T WAIT FOR ME AT THE GATE..
WE DON'T HAVE A GATE..
IT'S EMBARRASSING TO WAIT FOR SOMEONE WHEN YOU DON'T HAVE A GATE..
SCHULZ

HERE, I NEED YOU TO TEST ME ON THESE HISTORICAL DATES..
IN WHAT YEAR DID THE VISIGOTHS CROSS THE DANUBE?
WHO CARES?
I'VE ALWAYS BEEN GOOD WITH HISTORICAL DATES..
SCHULZ

BING ♫
♫ BONG
FOOTBALL TIME AGAIN, CHUCK!
SCHULZ

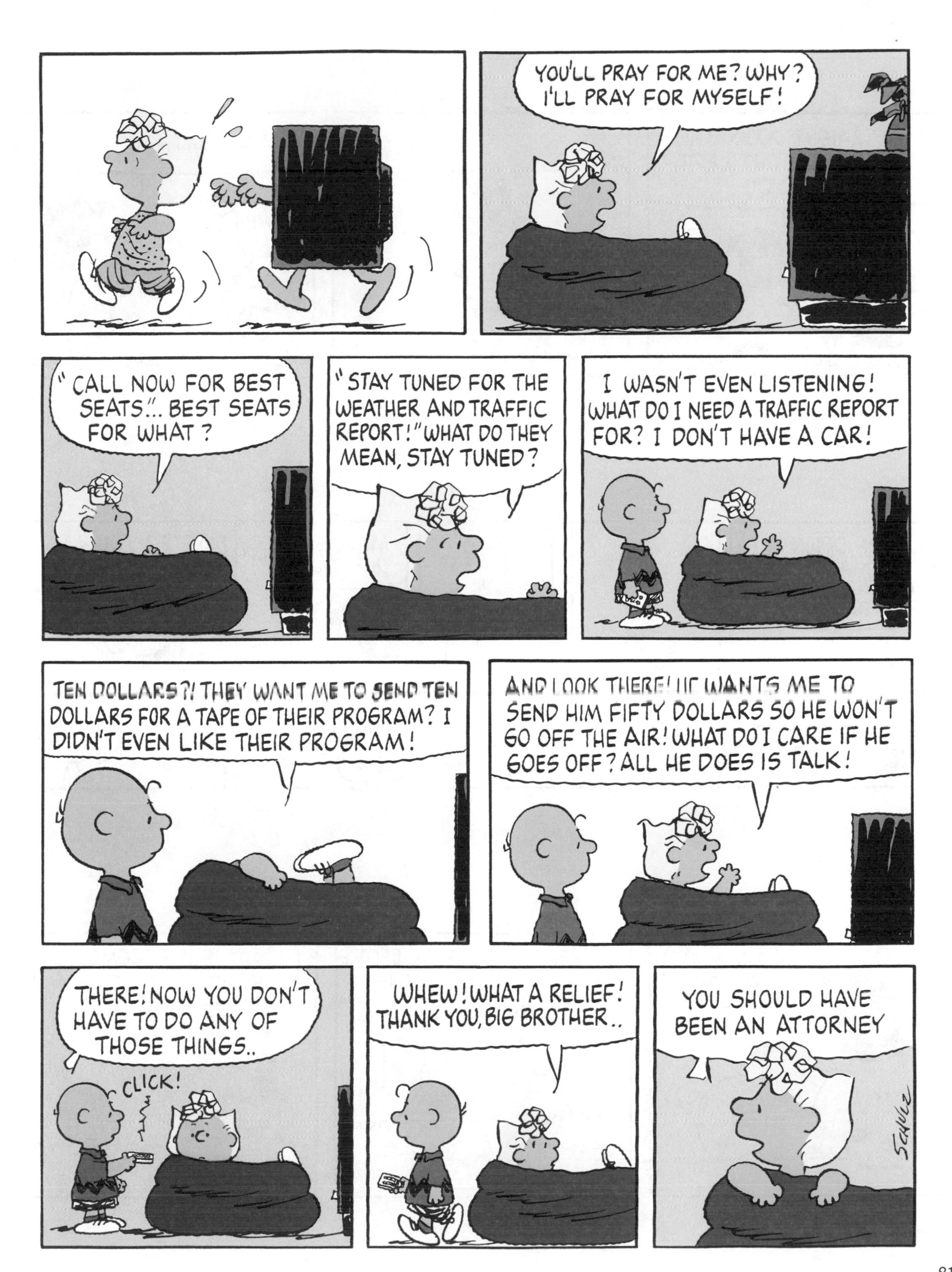

YOU'LL PRAY FOR ME? WHY? I'LL PRAY FOR MYSELF!
"CALL NOW FOR BEST SEATS."... BEST SEATS FOR WHAT?
"STAY TUNED FOR THE WEATHER AND TRAFFIC REPORT!" WHAT DO THEY MEAN, STAY TUNED?
I WASN'T EVEN LISTENING! WHAT DO I NEED A TRAFFIC REPORT FOR? I DON'T HAVE A CAR!
TEN DOLLARS?! THEY WANT ME TO SEND TEN DOLLARS FOR A TAPE OF THEIR PROGRAM? I DIDN'T EVEN LIKE THEIR PROGRAM!
AND LOOK THERE! HE WANTS ME TO SEND HIM FIFTY DOLLARS SO HE WON'T GO OFF THE AIR! WHAT DO I CARE IF HE GOES OFF? ALL HE DOES IS TALK!
THERE! NOW YOU DON'T HAVE TO DO ANY OF THOSE THINGS..
CLICK!
WHEW! WHAT A RELIEF! THANK YOU, BIG BROTHER..
YOU SHOULD HAVE BEEN AN ATTORNEY
SCHULZ

GO STRAIGHT DOWN THE FIELD, MARCIE, CUT LEFT, AND I'LL HIT YOU..

HIT ME WITH WHAT ?
SCHULZ

I'LL RUN DOWN THE FIELD, MARCIE, AND YOU THROW ME THE BALL..
?
MARCIE! WHERE DID YOU GO?!
AFTER YOU RAN DOWN THE FIELD, I SUDDENLY FELT VERY LONELY..
SCHULZ

ARE YOU READY?
I'M READY, MARCIE, BUT BEFORE YOU KICK THE BALL, SQUEEZE IT A FEW TIMES...
WHAT IF IT BECOMES FOND OF ME?
SCHULZ

MY DAD BOUGHT ME THIS HELMET, SIR.. HE SAYS GIRLS CAN PLAY SPORTS JUST AS WELL AS BOYS CAN..

I TRIED IT IN THE POOL, AND I ALMOST DROWNED..

YOU THINK YOU'RE VERY CLEVER, DON'T YOU?

SCHOOL STARTED LAST WEEK!!
I WASN'T SURE YOU HAD NOTICED

SUPPERTIME!
SUPPERTIME?
YEAHH! IT'S SUPPERTIME!!
HERE WE GO AGAIN..ALL THAT DANCING AROUND..
SUPPERTIME!
SUPP.. SUPP.. SUPPERTIME!
AND THEN HE ALWAYS EXPECTS ME TO JOIN IN..
..AND I'VE NEVER LEARNED THE TEXAS TWO-STEP
SLOW, SLOW, QUICK, QUICK!
SCHULZ

MY DAD TOOK ME TO MY FIRST HOCKEY GAME LAST NIGHT..
IT WAS REALLY GREAT..
I LOVED WATCHING THE ZAMBONI GO AROUND..
YOU'RE VERY WEIRD, MARCIE..
SCHULZ

GRAMMA SAYS THAT JUST BEFORE SHE GOES TO SLEEP EACH NIGHT, SHE HEARS ANGELS SINGING..
I HEARD SOMETHING LIKE THAT MYSELF LAST NIGHT...
YOU HEARD ANGELS SINGING?
NO, MY DOG WANTED TO COME IN..
SCHULZ

I CAN'T REMEMBER MY LOCKER COMBINATION
WE DON'T HAVE LOCKERS IN OUR SCHOOL..
US MAIL
THAT WAS ANOTHER THING I COULDN'T REMEMBER
SCHULZ

I KNOW YOU'RE THINKING OF GRABBING THIS BLANKET, AND DRAGGING ME ALL OVER THE NEIGHBORHOOD
THEREFORE, I WOULD SUGGEST YOU PUT THAT THOUGHT IN THE DEEPEST RECESS OF YOUR MIND..
DOGS' MINDS DON'T HAVE RECESSES!
SCHULZ

FINESSE!
SCHULZ

MY DAD TOOK ME TO ANOTHER HOCKEY GAME LAST NIGHT..
I GOT TO MEET THE MAN WHO DRIVES THE ZUCCHINI..
ZAMBONI..
WHATEVER
SCHULZ

AND THEN I WAS WONDERING WHY PEOPLE BECOME ATTORNEYS..
THAT'S WHERE THE COOKIES ARE..
I HEAR WE'RE NOT SUPPOSED TO JOKE ABOUT ATTORNEYS ANYMORE..
WHY IS THIS?
IS IT BECAUSE YOU'RE MORE SENSITIVE THAN YOU USED TO BE?
HEY! GET A LOAD OF THE FUNNY LOOKING ATTORNEY! HE'S DRESSED IN A DOG SUIT!
WHAT ARE YOU GONNA TRY TO DO, MISTER ATTORNEY, FOOL THE JUDGE?
WHAP!!
I GUESS YOU ARE SENSITIVE, AREN'T YOU?
ATTORNEYS ARE BORN SENSITIVE
SCHULZ

I'M AWAKE!
BUT I CAN'T GET DRESSED RIGHT AWAY..
MY SOCKS ARE STILL SLEEPING

Z
Z
Z
Z
Z
U.S. MAIL
WHY DO I HAVE THE FEELING THE SCHOOL BUS HAS BROKEN DOWN AGAIN?

I THINK I'LL ASK THE TEACHER IF I CAN MOVE MY DESK NEXT TO THAT LITTLE RED-HAIRED GIRL..
THEN, ONE DAY I CAN REACH OVER AND TOUCH HER HAND..
AND SHE CAN LOOK AT ME LIKE I'VE LOST MY MIND!
MAYBE I'LL ASK THE TEACHER IF I CAN MOVE MY DESK OUT INTO THE HALLWAY..

OKAY, MARCIE, WHEN I COME RUNNING DOWN THE FIELD, YOU TRY TO STOP ME..
AND DON'T FORGET TO USE YOUR HELMET..
BONK!
THANKS FOR THE SUGGESTION, SIR!

YOU DIDN'T KNOW THAT THE EARTH ROTATES?
WELL, I SUPPOSE THERE ARE A LOT OF THINGS YOU DON'T HAVE TO KNOW IF YOU'RE A BIRD..
LIFE IS MORE DIFFICULT FOR DOGS.. WE'RE REQUIRED TO KNOW EVERYTHING
YES, MOST OF US REMAIN QUITE HUMBLE..

PLEASE, YOU DON'T HAVE TO TELL ME EVERY LITTLE DETAIL!

OVER HERE!
THIS IS A BRAND NEW BALL, CHARLIE BROWN! I'LL HOLD IT, AND YOU COME RUNNING UP, AND KICK IT!
A BRAND NEW BALL! WOW!
THIS IS A REAL TREAT!
AAUGH!
WUMP
IT SUDDENLY OCCURRED TO ME THAT IF I LET YOU KICK IT, IT WOULDN'T BE NEW ANYMORE..
SCHULZ

YES, MA'AM.. THE ANSWER IS "TWELVE"
IT IS? I WAS RIGHT?
TAKE IT EASY, MA'AM..
SPLASH A LITTLE COLD WATER ON YOUR FACE, AND YOU'LL FEEL BETTER..

IF YOU REALLY LOVED ME, YOU'D BUY ME A MUSIC BOX..
IF YOU REALLY LOVED ME, YOU WOULDN'T ASK ME TO BUY YOU A MUSIC BOX..
ANOTHER TIE

I THINK A MUSIC BOX IS THE MOST ROMANTIC GIFT THAT A BOY CAN GIVE TO A GIRL..
HOW ABOUT HALF OF A PEANUT BUTTER SANDWICH?
WHAT SONG DOES IT PLAY?

A MUSIC BOX! LINUS, YOU BOUGHT ME A MUSIC BOX!
WELL, YOU SAID A MUSIC BOX IS THE MOST ROMANTIC GIFT THAT A BOY CAN GIVE TO A GIRL..
IT IS! IT'S VERY SPECIAL..
I'LL PUT IT WITH ALL THE OTHERS
SCHULZ

SCHULZ
OKAY, GO LEAN ON A CAT!

I NEED YOU TO WRITE A THEME FOR ME..
IF YOU DON'T WRITE IT YOURSELF, HOW WILL YOU EVER LEARN?
LEARN?
SCHULZ

YES, MA'AM..I'M READY...
THIS IS MY REPORT ON AUTUMN..
WHEN AUTUMN COMES, THE LEAVES BEGIN TO FALL...
NOW, I NEED A VOLUNTEER FROM THE CLASS..HOW ABOUT YOU? THE STUPID LOOKING KID IN THE FRONT ROW..
ALL RIGHT, LET'S SAY THIS KID IS WALKING THROUGH THE WOODS..
SUDDENLY, THE LEAVES BEGIN TO FALL..
IT'S AUTUMN !!
THANKS, KID! YOU WERE GREAT! JUST STAY AWAY FROM ANYONE WHO HAS A RAKE..

Dear Brother Snoopy,
Life here on the desert is exciting.

Last night the sun went down and this morning the sun came up.

There's always something happening.

SCHULZ

Z
AFRICA! SIXTEEN! SHAKESPEARE! ALABAMA! THE RIVER NILE!
WERE ANY OF THOSE RIGHT, MA'AM? I COULD TELL HER WHEN SHE WAKES UP AGAIN..
Z
SCHULZ

I'M READY, SIR..
LET'S GO OUT AND KICK THAT BALL AROUND ON THE OL' GRIDLOCK!
GRIDIRON, MARCIE..
WHATEVER
SCHULZ

SOMEDAY I WANT TO GO OVER TO JERICHO, AND WATCH THE WALLS COME TUMBLING DOWN
I THINK YOU'RE ABOUT THREE THOUSAND YEARS TOO LATE..
RATS! NOBODY EVER TELLS ME ANYTHING!
SCHULZ

NOTHING IS MORE EMPTY THAN AN EMPTY MAILBOX..
IF YOU PUT YOUR EAR UP REAL CLOSE, YOU CAN HEAR THE OCEAN ROAR..
SCHULZ

I THINK SOUNDS ARE INTERESTING, DON'T YOU?
WHAT IS YOUR FAVORITE SOUND?
KLUNK
"KLUNK"? YES, "KLUNK" IS A VERY INTERESTING SOUND..
SCHULZ

SIR, INSTEAD OF PLAYING, MAYBE I SHOULD JUST BE A CHEERLEADER..
LISTEN TO THIS...
COME ON, TEAM! TRY TO DO YOUR VERY BEST!!
A LITTLE TOO IMPASSIONED, HUH?
LET'S JUST WORK ON SOME MORE PLAYS, MARCIE
SCHULZ

"FIGHT, FIGHT, FIGHT WITH ALL YOUR MIGHT, AND GO ON TO A HIGHER HEIGHT!"
MARCIE, THAT'S THE WORST CHEER I'VE EVER HEARD!
I HAD HOPED IT WOULD BE INSPIRATIONAL, SIR..
IT'LL INSPIRE EVERYONE TO GO HOME..
HOW ABOUT, "TURN OUT THE LIGHTS, LUNCH IS OVER"?
SCHULZ

HEY, CHUCK.. I WAS WONDERING IF YOU NEED A CHEERLEADER FOR YOUR FOOTBALL TEAM..
STUPID MARCIE HERE THINKS SHE CAN BE A CHEERLEADER..
SORRY, I ALREADY HAVE ONE..
"WOOF WOOF! ARF ARF! LET'S GET 'EM IN THE SECOND HARF!"
SCHULZ

SCHULZ
THIS GAME IS GOING INTO OVERTIME..
IT MUST BE MIDNIGHT WHERE THEY'RE PLAYING..
I'M SURPRISED THE CROWD IS STILL THERE..
THEY SHOULD GO HOME AND FEED THEIR DOG..

EDITORIAL QUEEN
It was a dark and stormy night
Suddenly, a shot rang out.
LET ME SEE WHAT YOU'VE WRITTEN SO FAR..
YOU KNOW, WHEN YOU'RE WRITING A STORY, IT'S VERY IMPORTANT TO SELECT THE PERFECT WORDS...
IN THIS CASE, I WONDER IF "SUDDENLY" IS THE RIGHT WORD..
Gradually, a shot rang out.
SCHULZ

I GOT A "C," AN "A," AN "R" AND A "D"! ..NOT TOO BAD, HUH, MARCIE?
THAT'S "CARD," SIR... IT SAYS "REPORT CARD"
I WAS WONDERING HOW I GOT AN "R"...
SCHULZ

THE LOCH NESS PUTTER!
SCHULZ

WHERE ARE YOU GOING?
OUT TO MAKE MONEY RAKING LEAVES..
I'M GOING TO USE SALESMANSHIP..I'LL CONVINCE EVERYONE THEY NEED THEIR LEAVES RAKED!
IT'S ALL A MATTER OF SALESMANSHIP, PERSEVERANCE AND BEING WELL LIKED..
WILLY LOMAN OF THE LEAVES
SCHULZ

ASK YOUR DAD IF HE WANTS ME TO RAKE YOUR LEAVES..
HE SAYS, "HOW MUCH FOR JUST ONE LEAF ?"
MY DAD THINKS HE'S VERY FUNNY
SCHULZ

HOW DID IT GO? DID YOU MAKE ANY MONEY DOING LEAVES?
NO, NOT A PENNY..
MAYBE I CAN TRY IT..COULD I BORROW YOUR CLUB?
RAKE
WHATEVER
OKAY, HERE'S HOW IT WORKS..I RENT YOU THE RAKE, SEE, AND..
SCHULZ

HERE'S THE WORLD WAR I FLYING ACE SITTING IN A SMALL FRENCH CAFE.. THE WAR DRAGS ON... HE IS DEPRESSED..
CHARLES, YOUR DOG IS IN OUR KITCHEN AGAIN DRINKING ALL OUR ROOT BEER..
GENERAL PERSHING SAYS FOR YOU TO GET BACK TO THE AERODROME RIGHT AWAY..
PRESSURE AGAIN FROM HEADQUARTERS, RAIN AND MUD,... DESPAIR...
MOM!
SCHULZ

NOW WHAT?
EXPLAIN TO ME WHAT I'M DOING OUT HERE..
ON HALLOWEEN NIGHT, THE "GREAT PUMPKIN" RISES OUT OF THE PUMPKIN PATCH, AND BRINGS TOYS TO ALL THE CHILDREN IN THE WORLD!
JUST THINK..IF HE CHOOSES THIS PUMPKIN PATCH, YOU AND I WILL BE HERE TO SEE HIM!
LOOK! THERE HE IS! IT'S THE "GREAT PUMPKIN"!
THAT'S NOT THE "GREAT PUMPKIN"... THAT'S A DOG HOLDING A PUMPKIN ON A STICK!
EXPLAIN TO ME AGAIN WHAT I'M DOING OUT HERE..
TRICK OR TREAT!
SCHULZ

HERE'S THE WORLD WAR I FLYING ACE WALKING BACK TO THE AERODROME..
SUDDENLY HE SEES A LIGHT IN THE WINDOW OF A SMALL SHABBY FARM HOUSE
HE TAPS GENTLY ON THE DOOR..
BAM! BAM! BAM!!
GO ON HOME, YOU STUPID BEAGLE!
SOMETIMES THE UNIFORM FRIGHTENS THEM..
SCHULZ

BEFORE HE GETS BACK TO THE AERODROME, THE FLYING ACE FEELS HE NEEDS ONE MORE ROOT BEER..
HE ENTERS ANOTHER SMALL SEEDY CAFE, AND BECKONS TO THE PLAIN LOOKING WAITRESS...
HEY, CHUCK! YOUR DOG JUST WALKED INTO OUR HOUSE..
WELL, YEAH, HE SEEMED TO WANT SOMETHING TO DRINK..I GAVE HIM WHAT WE HAD...
PRETTY CHEAP ROOT BEER..
SCHULZ

OKAY, FLYING ACE.. YOU'VE HAD ENOUGH... YOU'D BETTER GET GOING..
SMAK!
PATHETIC CREATURE..SHE SEEMED RATHER LONELY..
SCHULZ

I WAS PASSING BY THIS QUAINT JOINT, AND HEARD THE TINKLING OF A PIANO..
PLAY "TIPPERARY" FOR ME, SON..I FEEL SORT OF DOWN TONIGHT...

HI, CHARLES..DID YOUR DOG GET HOME ALL RIGHT?
SURE, CHARLIE BROWN, HE ALMOST KICKED OUR DOOR DOWN!
HEY, CHUCK, THAT'S A WEIRD DOG YOU'VE GOT THERE!
SO ALL I'M SAYING IS I DON'T WANT HIM LEANING ON MY PIANO..
WHY CAN'T I HAVE A NORMAL DOG LIKE EVERYONE ELSE?
WAS THAT GENERAL PERSHING? TELL HIM I'M ON MY WAY..

IT IS DAWN.. HERE'S THE WORLD WAR I FLYING ACE WALKING ONTO THE AERODROME
HE CLIMBS INTO THE COCKPIT OF HIS SOPWITH CAMEL, AND ADJUSTS THE SUTTON HARNESS...
NOW, THE EARLY MORNING QUIET IS SHATTERED BY THE ROAR OF THE 110 HP LE RHÔNE ENGINE!
SOME PEOPLE HAVE DOGS WHO BARK A LOT, OR DIG HOLES IN THE GARDEN, OR...

AND DON'T FORGET YOUR LUNCH
GRAMPA SAYS HE USED TO WALK TEN MILES TO SCHOOL IN THE DEEP SNOW..
HA! LOOK AT THIS!
WAIT 'TIL I TELL HIM ABOUT TODAY! OH, BOY!
I'LL TELL HIM HOW IT STARTED TO SNOW WHILE WE WERE WAITING FOR THE SCHOOL BUS..
AND SUDDENLY IT TURNED INTO A BLIZZARD, AND THE BUS GOT STUCK IN HUGE SNOW DRIFTS..
AND ALL THE SCHOOLS HAD TO CLOSE, AND..
RATS!
SCHULZ

HERE'S THE WORLD WAR I FLYING ACE SEARCHING THE SKY FOR HIS ENEMY, THE RED BARON..
SUDDENLY, OUT OF NOWHERE, A HAIL OF BULLETS RIPS THE FABRIC OF HIS SOPWITH CAMEL!
WITH UNBELIEVABLE SKILL HE GUIDES THE STRICKEN CRAFT BACK TO THE AERODROME
FEARING A FIERY EXPLOSION, HE LEAPS FROM THE COCKPIT!
WHAT'S A SUPPER DISH DOING ON THE RUNWAY?!
SCHULZ

WHY DOES YOUR DOG STAND IN THE BACKYARD JUST STARING AT HIS DOGHOUSE ?
THAT STUPID RED BARON..LOOK WHAT HE DID TO MY PLANE...
SCHULZ

ON VETERANS DAY I ALWAYS GO OVER TO BILL MAULDIN'S HOUSE TO QUAFF A FEW ROOT BEERS..
BILL KNEW MY HERO, AUDIE MURPHY..
I'VE TOLD BILL HOW I MET CAPTAIN HARRY TRUMAN IN FRANCE...
BUT BILL NEVER BELIEVES ME..
SCHULZ

ARE YOU THROUGH WITH THE SPORTS SECTION?
WHY? YOU DON'T KNOW ANYTHING ABOUT SPORTS..
IS THERE AN "ANYTHING" SECTION FOR SOMEONE WHO DOESN'T KNOW ANYTHING ABOUT ANYTHING?
SCHULZ

SOMETIMES, I LIE AWAKE AT NIGHT, AND I ASK, "WHY ME?"
THEN A VOICE ANSWERS, "NOTHING PERSONAL.. YOUR NAME JUST HAPPENED TO COME UP.."
SCHULZ

TODAY?! THE TEST IS TODAY? YES, MA'AM, I'M SURPRISED..
I THOUGHT MAYBE BEFORE THE REAL TEST THERE'D BE A PRO-AM..
SCHULZ

WHAT HAPPENED TO HIM?
I THINK IT'S HAPPENED BEFORE..
HE GETS HYPNOTIZED WATCHING THE ZAMBONI GO AROUND..
SCHULZ

THIS CAN OF DOG FOOD COST EIGHTY-NINE CENTS..
THIS FROZEN DINNER YOU'RE HAVING TONIGHT COST THREE DOLLARS AND FIFTY CENTS..
MOM AND DAD SHOULD TRADE YOU IN FOR ANOTHER DOG..
STOP GRINNING
SCHULZ

MY DAD'S TAKING ME TO ANOTHER HOCKEY GAME TONIGHT..
I THINK WE'RE GOING TO SEE THE "MIGHTY FLAMINGOS"
"DUCKS," MARCIE
SOMETHING LIKE THAT..
DON'T GET RUN OVER BY THE ZUCCHINI..
ZAMBONI, SIR..
YOU'RE GETTING THERE, MARCIE
SCHULZ

THIS IS MY REPORT ON A REAL HOCKEY PUCK..
I GOT IT LAST NIGHT AT THE GAME WITH THE "MIGHTY FLAMINGOS"
MY DAD WANTED ME TO GET IT AUTOGRAPHED..
I TOLD HIM I THINK AUTOGRAPHING IS STUPID..
BESIDES, I SAID, YOU WERE THE ONE IT HIT ON THE HEAD!
SCHULZ

DID YOU KNOW IT TOOK LEO TOLSTOY SIX YEARS TO WRITE "WAR AND PEACE"?
I KNOW HOW HE MUST HAVE FELT..
I'VE BEEN WORKING ON THIS STORY NOW FOR OVER HALF AN HOUR..
SCHULZ

I NEED HELP WITH MY HOMEWORK
WHICH SUBJECT?
SUBJECT?
YOU MEAN WE HAVE SUBJECTS?
SCHULZ

I'VE DECIDED TO SPEND THE REST OF MY LIFE LOOKING FOR "THE BIG ROCK CANDY MOUNTAIN"
I DIDN'T FIND IT TODAY, BUT MAYBE I'LL FIND IT TOMORROW..
IF YOU REALLY WANT SOMETHING IN THIS LIFE, YOU HAVE TO BE DETERMINED!
IF I DON'T FIND IT TOMORROW, I THINK I'LL QUIT LOOKING..
SCHULZ

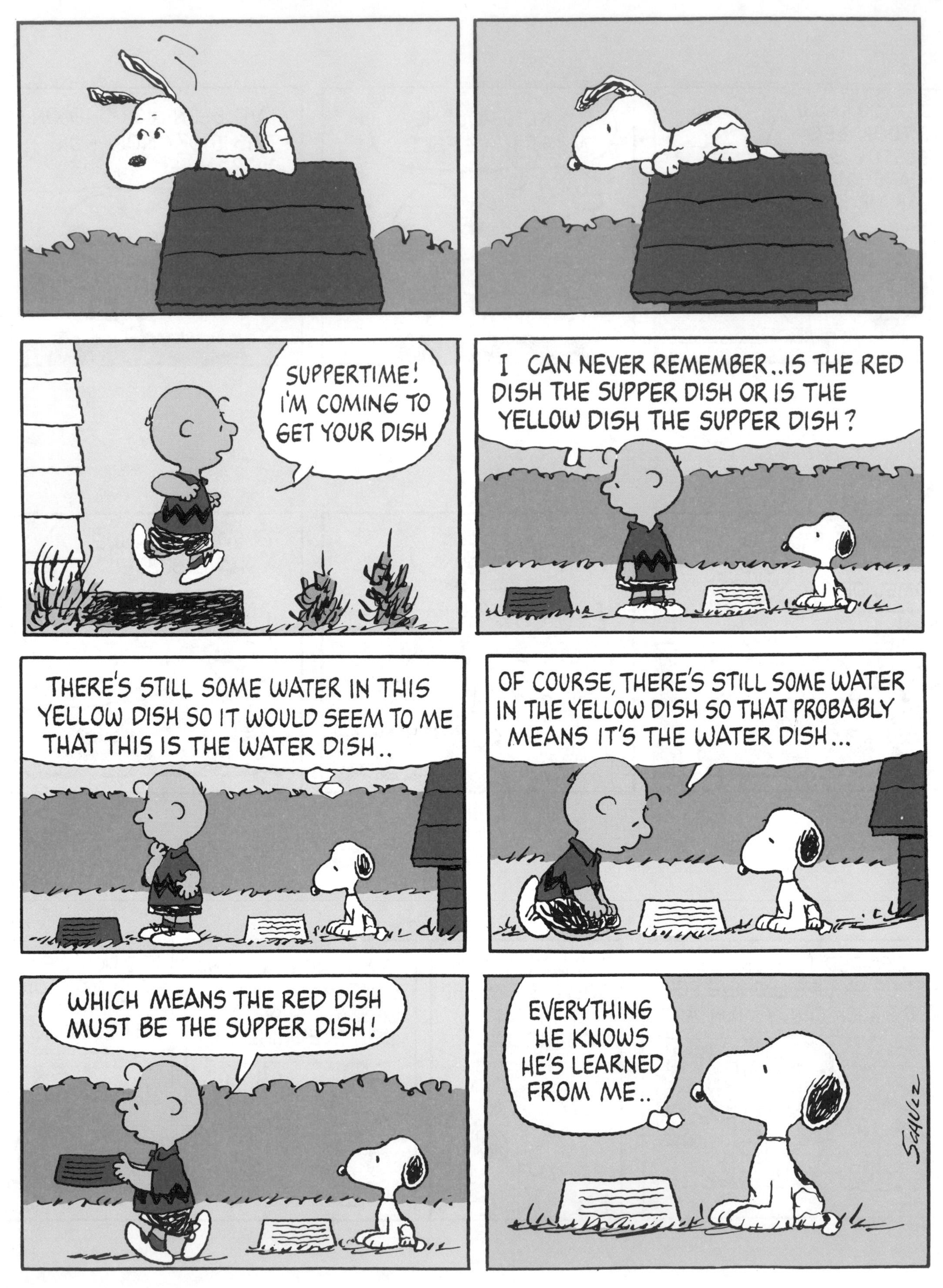
SUPPERTIME! I'M COMING TO GET YOUR DISH
I CAN NEVER REMEMBER..IS THE RED DISH THE SUPPER DISH OR IS THE YELLOW DISH THE SUPPER DISH?
THERE'S STILL SOME WATER IN THIS YELLOW DISH SO IT WOULD SEEM TO ME THAT THIS IS THE WATER DISH..
OF COURSE, THERE'S STILL SOME WATER IN THE YELLOW DISH SO THAT PROBABLY MEANS IT'S THE WATER DISH...
WHICH MEANS THE RED DISH MUST BE THE SUPPER DISH!
EVERYTHING HE KNOWS HE'S LEARNED FROM ME..
SCHULZ

HAS THE SCHOOL BUS COME YET?
WHY DON'T YOU OPEN YOUR EYES AND SEE FOR YOURSELF?
IT'S TOO EARLY IN THE MORNING TO GO TO ALL THAT TROUBLE..
SCHULZ

YES, MA'AM, I WALKED TO SCHOOL IN THE RAIN..
YES, MA'AM..MY WET HAIR IS DRIPPING ON THE DESK, AND THE WATER SEEMS TO BE RUNNING DOWN THE AISLE...
NO, MA'AM, IT'S THE KIDS BEHIND ME WHO ARE MAKING THE LITTLE PAPER SAILBOATS..
SCHULZ

THIS FOOTBALL LOOKS LIKE A THANKSGIVING TURKEY WITHOUT THE DRUMSTICKS..
CATCH THE TURKEY, SIR! WHITE MEAT OR DARK MEAT? SAVE ME THE WISHBONE!
THE TURKEY FELL OFF THE TABLE, SIR..
I HATE PLAYING WITH YOU, MARCIE!
SCHULZ

SURE, I CAN COUNT.. I SEE EIGHT FINGERS AND TWO THUMBS...
AND ONE NOSE, AND TWO EYES, AND ONE MOUTH, AND TWO EARS...
AND ONE BIG SISTER!

IT'S GOING TO BE COLD TONIGHT SO I THOUGHT YOU MIGHT WANT TO USE THIS BEDROLL..
THOUGHTFUL, BUT SORT OF USELESS..
SCHULZ

I WONDER IF THEY HAVE FRACTIONS IN HEAVEN..
NO FRACTIONS, SIR..NO DECIMALS, EITHER...
HOW ABOUT COMMAS?
THERE HAVE TO BE COMMAS, SIR.. WE CAN'T AVOID THEM
ETERNITY'S GOING TO BE LONGER THAN I THOUGHT..
SCHULZ

ARE WE THERE?
SCHULZ

WELL, I'LL BE! THIS IS THE SAME LITTLE BUG I SAW OVER ON THE PLAYGROUND TWO DAYS AGO..

HOW DO YOU KNOW?

I HAVE A GOOD MEMORY FOR FACES
SCHULZ

CAN YOU SEE THE SCHOOL BUS?
NOT YET
I'VE CHANGED MY MIND.. I DON'T THINK I'LL GET ON THE BUS..
WHY NOT?
SCHULZ
MY LUNCH JUST WENT HOME..

HEY, CHUCK, HOW ABOUT A FOOTBALL GAME TOMORROW?
YOU KNOW, A REGULAR STRAIGHT AHEAD, DOWN IN THE DIRT, IN YOUR FACE, ROCK 'EM, SOCK 'EM, ANYTHING GOES, GOOD OLD FASHIONED FOOTBALL GAME!
IS THE LIBRARY OPEN TOMORROW?
SCHULZ

OKAY, CHUCK..HEADS OR TAILS...YOU CALL IT..
TELL YOUR PLAYER TO WAIT 'TIL THE COIN COMES DOWN!
SCHULZ

GET READY, MARCIE.. HERE COMES THE KICKOFF..
I'M READY, SIR..RESEARCH SHOWS THAT IF A GIRL DOES NOT PARTICIPATE IN SPORTS BY THE TIME SHE'S TEN, SHE PROBABLY WON'T WHEN SHE'S THIRTY-FIVE..
BONK!
YOU'LL NEVER BE THIRTY-FIVE, MARCIE..
SCHULZ

OKAY, FRANKLIN, GO STRAIGHT OUT, THEN CUT RIGHT, AND I'LL HIT YOU WITH THE BOMB..
AREN'T YOU ON THE OTHER TEAM, SWEETIE?
MY GLASSES ARE WET..I CAN'T SEE A THING..
SCHULZ

..SO WHAT WE'RE TALKING ABOUT HERE IS EMPOWERMENT THROUGH INNER DIALOGUE HOPEFULLY LEADING TO LIFE ENHANCEMENT..
SCHULZ

WHERE AM I?
WHO'S GOT THE BALL?
SOMEBODY CALL THE VET!
IS IT STILL RAINING OR AM I BLEEDING?
ISN'T THIS GREAT, CHUCK? GOOD OLD FASHIONED, DOWN IN THE DIRT FOOTBALL!

WE'RE NOT LETTING A LITTLE RAIN SPOIL OUR FUN, ARE WE, CHUCK?
DID SHE SAY "RAIN" OR "PAIN"?

THANKS FOR THE GAME, CHUCK! I HAD LOTS OF FUN..YOU GUYS HAD FUN, TOO, DIDN'T YOU?
LOTS OF FUN..
FROM NOW ON I'M GOING TO BE A HOUSE DOG..

BOY, AFTER A GAME LIKE THAT IT'D BE NICE TO SIT IN A HOT TUB..
I'LL SAY IT WOULD..
A LOT BETTER THAN A COLD WATER DISH
SCHULZ

WASN'T THAT FUN, MARCIE? GOOD OLD FASHIONED, PLAY IN THE RAIN, DOWN IN THE DIRT, FOOTBALL!
I THINK I LOST MY SHOES..
AND NOW IT'S STARTING TO SNOW! WE SHOULD PLAY AGAIN TOMORROW..
I NEVER KNEW LIFE COULD BE SO BEAUTIFUL!
SCHULZ

IF YOU'RE COLLECTING FOR CHARITY, WHAT CHARITY ARE YOU COLLECTING FOR?
SCHULZ

MERCI!
WELL, LOOK HERE! IT'S SANTA! THIS IS MY LITTLE BROTHER "RERUN," SANTA...
TELL SANTA WHAT YOU WANT FOR CHRISTMAS, "RERUN"..
WELL, I'D LIKE SOME BOOKS, A VIDEO GAME, SOME IN-LINE SKATES AND MAYBE A NICE SWEATER..
THAT WAS GREAT, "RERUN"..NOW YOU HAVE SOMETHING TO LOOK FORWARD TO ON CHRISTMAS MORNING..
BEFORE WE GO ANY FARTHER, COULD I ASK YOU SOMETHING?
DID YOU KNOW I WAS TALKING TO A DOG?
SCHULZ

I HAVE TO READ A BOOK DURING CHRISTMAS VACATION..
TRY THIS ONE.. IT'S A REAL PAGE-TURNER
I HATE TURNING PAGES
SCHULZ

THIS IS THE BOOK I HAVE TO READ FOR SCHOOL..I WANT YOU TO READ IT FOR ME..
YOU MEAN I'M SUPPOSED TO READ IT WHILE YOU JUST SIT HERE AND LISTEN..
SCHULZ
LISTEN ?

ALL RIGHT, I READ YOUR BOOK FOR YOU... NOW, WHAT DO I DO ?
NOW, YOU WRITE THE REPORT..
I HOPE YOU APPRECIATE ALL THIS..
I'LL SEND YOU A CHRISTMAS CARD
SCHULZ

ALL RIGHT, I WROTE YOUR BOOK REPORT FOR YOU.. SEE WHAT YOU THINK..
"THIS WAS THE MOST EXCITING BOOK I HAVE EVER READ..I LIKED ALL THE CHARACTERS"
"THE DESCRIPTIONS WERE BEAUTIFUL, AND THE STORY VERY SUSPENSEFUL"
I DON'T KNOW..IF I HAD READ IT, I WOULDN'T HAVE LIKED IT THAT MUCH
SCHULZ

BEND DOWN..
SCHULZ

ONE OF THE GREAT JOYS IN LIFE IS SLIDING ON AN ICY SIDEWALK..
JOE 'ICE FOLLIES'..
SCHULZ

WELL, A BICYCLE WOULD BE NICE..
AND MAYBE A NEW SLED AND A PAIR OF IN-LINE SKATES..
AND MAYBE A JUMP ROPE..
IT'S NICE TO BE ABLE TO TELL SANTA CLAUS WHAT YOU WANT FOR CHRISTMAS, ISN'T IT?
IF YOU CAN GET PAST THE SECRETARY..

YES, MA'AM..IT'S COLD OUTSIDE...
I'D LIKE AN ICE CREAM CONE, PLEASE
DO YOU MIND MITTEN MONEY? THIS IS SOME MONEY THAT'S BEEN IN MY MITTEN SINCE LAST WINTER..
ONE MORE QUESTION..
HOW DO YOU EAT ICE CREAM THROUGH A WOOLEN SCARF?
SCHULZ

WHERE'S MY BIG FURRY HAT?
HAS ANYONE SEEN MY BIG FURRY HAT?
SCHULZ

I THINK I'VE LEARNED SOMETHING
YOU CAN SLIDE DOWN THE STEPS..
BUT YOU CAN'T SLIDE..
UP THE STEPS..
SCHULZ

MERRY CHRISTMAS

WHAT ARE YOU DOING?
I'M WRITING A "THANK YOU" LETTER..WHAT DID I GET FROM GRAMMA FOR CHRISTMAS?
WHICH GRAMMA? YOU'VE GOT TWO OF THEM..
MAYBE I'LL WRITE TO GRAMPA.. WHAT DID I GET FROM GRAMPA?
WHICH GRAMPA? YOU'VE GOT TWO OF 'EM..
WHAT DID I GET FROM MY AUNT? MAYBE I'LL WRITE TO MY AUNT...
DOWN BY THE RIVER
WHICH AUNT? YOU'VE GOT FIVE OF THEM..
DOWN BY THE RIVER
WHAT DID I GET FROM MY THIRD COUSIN ONCE-REMOVED?
SCHULZ

The Dog - That Most Magnificent of All Creatures.
WHAT KIND OF DOG ARE YOU TALKING ABOUT?
Any Dog
SCHULZ

I'VE ALWAYS WONDERED HOW THE ZAMBONI GOT OFF THE ICE..
SCHULZ

" DR. MORTIMER'S VOICE SANK ALMOST TO A WHISPER, AND HE SAID, 'MR. HOLMES, THEY WERE THE FOOTPRINTS OF A GIGANTIC HOUND!' "
WELL, THAT'S ENOUGH READING FOR TONIGHT..
AND I NEVER SLEEP AGAIN FOR THE REST OF MY LIFE..
SCHULZ

SHALL WE READ SOME MORE OF "THE HOUND OF THE BASKERVILLES" TONIGHT ?
OKAY, I'M READY..
SCHULZ

The New Year had finally come.
In spite of all that had happened, he knew he had much to be thankful for.
He was still a dog.
SCHULZ

DID YOU MISS ME DURING CHRISTMAS VACATION ?
DID YOU GIVE ME A CHRISTMAS PRESENT ?
NO
SCHULZ
I DIDN'T MISS YOU

WOW!
YES, MA'AM ..WHAT YOU JUST TOLD US ABOUT THE STARS AND THE PLANETS IS REALLY FASCINATING..
AND YOU KNOW WHO'S INTERESTED IN THIS SORT OF THING?
MY DOG! YES, HE REALLY IS!
SO WHAT I'D LIKE TO DO RIGHT NOW IS RUN HOME, AND TELL HIM ALL ABOUT WHAT YOU JUST TAUGHT US...
YES, MA'AM..
NICE TRY, CHARLIE BROWN
SCHULZ

AFTER THAT, HOW LONG WAS IT BEFORE YOU SAW YOUR GRANDFATHER AGAIN ?
SCHULZ

LOOK HERE.. THERE'S A TINY LITTLE BOOK ON THE BOTTOM OF THE BIRD CAGE...
IT'S A DIARY! YOUR GRANDFATHER KEPT A DIARY WHILE HE WAS IN THE CAGE!
"I'VE BEEN IN HERE FOR SIX WEEKS NOW, AND MY ATTORNEY HAS NEVER CALLED BACK.."

YOUR GRANDFATHER WAS AMAZING..HE KEPT A DIARY ALL THE TIME HE WAS IN THE BIRD CAGE...
"MONDAY: I HATE IT IN HERE!"
"TUESDAY: I HATE IT IN HERE!"
"WEDNESDAY: I HATE IT IN HERE!"
NO, I DON'T THINK HE LIKED IT IN THERE..
SCHULZ

YOUR GRAMPA WROTE A LOT IN HIS DIARY..
"WHY AM I IN THIS CAGE? I NEVER DID ANYTHING WRONG..I HATE IT IN HERE! I SHOULD BE OUTSIDE FLYING AROUND LIKE OTHER BIRDS!"
SCHULZ

"ONCE A WEEK, THEY PUT MY CAGE OUTSIDE IN THE SUN..SOONER OR LATER THEY'RE GOING TO LEAVE THAT LITTLE DOOR OPEN.."
"ANYWAY, THIS IS A STUPID LIFE SITTING HERE ALONE WAITING FOR THAT TO.."
AND THAT'S IT! THE DIARY ENDS RIGHT THERE!
HE PROBABLY GOT OUT, AND IS SITTING ON A TELEPHONE WIRE RIGHT NOW LOOKING DOWN AT US...
EVERY TIME YOU SEE A BIRD SITTING ON A TELEPHONE WIRE, YOU SHOULD WAVE..IT MIGHT BE YOUR GRAMPA!
SCHULZ

"ALL'S RIGHT WITH THE WORLD"
WHAT DO PEOPLE MEAN WHEN THEY SAY, "ALL'S RIGHT WITH THE WORLD"?
SCHULZ
LUCY'S HERE

BOOT!
YOU DID WHAT?
WELL, IT COULD BE A MISDEMEANOR OR A FELONY..
KLUNK!
BUT MOST LIKELY IT COULD BE CONSIDERED MAYHEM
KLUNK!
MAYHEM IS "DEPRIVING A HUMAN BEING OF A MEMBER OF HIS BODY.." IN THIS CASE, HIS HEAD, RIGHT ?
NOW, A SNOWMAN ISN'T A HUMAN BEING SO I THINK WE..
KLUNK!
HOW CAN YOU TALK TO A CLIENT WHO KEEPS FAINTING ALL THE TIME ?
SCHULZ

THAT ZAMBONI MAKES GOOD ICE..

I HAVE TO DO A BOOK REPORT ON ZECHARIAH
GOOD FOR YOU..
IN A UNIQUE WAY, ZECHARIAH IS ONE OF THE MOST IMPORTANT BOOKS IN THE OLD TESTAMENT..
IF YOU NEED ANY HELP, JUST LET ME KNOW
HOW DO YOU SPELL IT?

WHEN I LEFT FOR SCHOOL THIS MORNING, YOU WERE ASLEEP..
WHEN I CAME HOME, YOU WERE STILL ASLEEP..
I FIND THAT INTERESTING, DON'T YOU?
I CAN'T HEAR YOU..I'M ASLEEP..

MY DAD AND I WENT TO ANOTHER HOCKEY GAME LAST NIGHT..
IT'S AMAZING HOW FAST THE PLAYERS SKATE UP AND DOWN THE COURT..
RINK
NEXT WEEK WE'RE GOING TO A BASKETBALL RINK

"IF YOU GIVE A MOUSE A COOKIE"
YOU SHOULD WRITE A BOOK LIKE THAT..
"If You Give a Beagle a Brownie"

HOW DO I LOOK? I'M GOING DOWN TO HAVE MY PICTURE TAKEN WITH SANTA CLAUS..
I THINK YOU'RE EITHER ABOUT THREE WEEKS TOO LATE OR MAYBE ELEVEN MONTHS TOO EARLY..
I'LL GO NOW, AND BE THE FIRST ONE IN LINE

"PETANQUE"?
BONJOUR, CAPITAINE!
DOES THE WORLD WAR I FLYING ACE KNOW HOW TO PLAY "PETANQUE"? THEN, I SHALL SHOW HIM..
"PETANQUE" ORIGINATED IN PROVENCE IN 1910..
WE BEGIN BY TOSSING A SMALL WOODEN BALL AHEAD OF US CALLED THE "COCHONNET"
YOU WILL THEN PITCH THIS HEAVY METAL "BOULE" AS CLOSE TO THE "COCHONNET" AS YOU CAN..
OF COURSE, YOU MUST BE CAREFUL NOT TO DROP THE HEAVY "BOULE" ON YOUR..
YIPE!
THE FLYING ACE IS RETURNED TO THE FIELD HOSPITAL..
?
"WHAT DID YOU DO IN THE GREAT WAR, GRAMPA?"
"I WAS WOUNDED PLAYING 'PETANQUE'"
SCHULZ

ON THE OTHER HAND, MAYBE I SHOULD GO GET MY CAMERA
SCHULZ

OH, NO! I LEFT MY LUNCH ON THE CURB..
DO YOU THINK THE BUS DRIVER WOULD TURN AROUND AND GO BACK SO I COULD GET IT?
MAYBE, IF YOU ASKED HIM NICELY..
HEY, MAC!
SCHULZ

WHEN PEOPLE WALK BY, AND LOOK IN OUR YARD, I THINK THEY SHOULD SEE A HAPPY DOG..
RIGHT NOW, NOBODY'S LOOKING...
YOU CAN PUT AWAY THE TAMBOURINE..
SCHULZ

IT SAYS HERE THAT THE AVERAGE CHILD WEARS DOWN 730 CRAYONS BEFORE HE OR SHE IS TEN YEARS OLD..
AND THAT COLORING PROMOTES UNDERSTANDING, AND BRINGS CHILDREN CLOSER TOGETHER..
WHAT COLOR SHOULD I MAKE THE SKY?
BLUE, YOU BLOCKHEAD!
SCHULZ

I'VE DEVELOPED A NEW IMPROVED PHILOSOPHY..
"WHO CARES? HOW SHOULD I KNOW? DO YOU THINK I'M OUT OF MY MIND?"
A GOOD PHILOSOPHY HELPS YOU ENDURE ALL OF THE TROUBLES WE HAVE IN LIFE..
"WHO CARES? HOW SHOULD I KNOW? DO YOU THINK I'M OUT OUT OF MY MIND?"
SCHULZ

OH, I SEE.. IT WAS A TRICK QUESTION, WASN'T IT?
NO WONDER I GOT IT WRONG..
CONGRATULATIONS, MA'AM.. YOU DID IT AGAIN!
SCHULZ

SORRY
NO MORE SLIDING DOWNHILL IN A CARDBOARD BOX..
NOW I HAVE A REAL SLED!
THE FASTEST SLED IN THE WORLD!
NOBODY WILL BE ABLE TO BEAT ME!
NOBODY!
SCHULZ

THE RAIN IS GETTING MY HOMEWORK ALL WET
I DIDN'T KNOW YOU HAD DONE ANY HOMEWORK
IF I HAD DONE MY HOMEWORK, THE RAIN WOULD BE GETTING IT ALL WET
SCHULZ

I'VE BEEN FEELING SORT OF LONELY LATELY..
YOU NEED SOME NEW FRIENDS, CHARLIE BROWN, OR A GOOD DOG..
I ALREADY HAVE A DOG..
I SAID A GOOD DOG
DON'T WALK SO FAST.. I'M TRYING TO BITE YOUR LEG!
SCHULZ

YOU'RE RIGHT..IT IS A LITTLE MORE WINDY TODAY THAN USUAL..
SCHULZ

"SILVER BLAZE" BY A. CONAN DOYLE
"..THE CURIOUS INCIDENT OF THE DOG IN THE NIGHTTIME." "THE DOG DID NOTHING IN THE NIGHTTIME." "THAT WAS THE CURIOUS INCIDENT," REMARKED SHERLOCK HOLMES...
MY FAVORITE PART..
SCHULZ

NOTHING WOULD MAKE ME HAPPIER THAN TO SEE YOU THROW THAT STUPID BLANKET AWAY..
BACKSPIN!
SCHULZ

WHEN YOU WRITE LIKE THAT, DO YOU EVER GET INK ON YOUR FINGERS?

WHAT?
SCHULZ

EAT
AH! A CUSTOMER!
GOOD EVENING, SIR.. WELCOME TO AN HOUR OF FINE DINING..
I THINK YOU'RE GOING TO BE VERY PLEASED WITH OUR SPECIAL FOOD AND SPECIAL SERVICE..
OF COURSE, OUR SPECIAL TONIGHT IS DOG FOOD..
I SHALL NOW GO TO THE KITCHEN, AND PERSONALLY PREPARE YOUR SPECIAL MEAL
YOU'RE GOING TO BE GLAD YOU CAME TO SUCH A SPECIAL PLACE..
IF THIS IS SUCH A SPECIAL PLACE, WHY AM I THE ONLY ONE HERE?
SCHULZ

HOW DO YOU THINK I'M DOING, MARCIE? CHECK THESE ANSWERS
YOU GOT THE FIRST NINE QUESTIONS WRONG, SIR..
OH, WELL.. I LEARNED A LONG TIME AGO THAT IT'S NOT HOW YOU START, IT'S HOW YOU FINISH..
YOU GOT THE LAST ONE WRONG, TOO!

THIS IS MY REPORT ON THE GUY WHO THOUGHT IT UP..
MA'AM?
THE TELEPHONE
ALEXANDER GRAHAM BELL..INVENTED? YES, MA'AM..THE TELEPHONE...
THIS IS MY REPORT ON THE GUY WHO THOUGHT IT UP..

AND THEN ALEXANDER GRAHAM BELL GOES, "OH, NO!"
AND THEN HE GOES, "MR. WATSON, COME HERE!" AND MR. WATSON GOES, "THAT'S IT!"
MA'AM?
AND THE TEACHER GOES, "D-MINUS!"
DON'T BUG ME, MARCIE!

I'VE DECIDED TO TIE A PINK RIBBON AROUND ALL MY LOVE LETTERS..
SEE? I ALREADY HAVE THE RIBBON..
BUT I DON'T HAVE ANY LOVE LETTERS..
SCHULZ

THERE'S NOTHING MORE PATHETIC THAN A LITTLE DOG SITTING IN THE RAIN..
THERE'S NOTHING MORE PATHETIC THAN A DOG TOO STUPID TO GET IN OUT OF THE RAIN..
EITHER WAY I'M PATHETIC..
SCHULZ

SOMETIMES I LIE AWAKE AT NIGHT, AND I ASK, "WHY AM I HERE?"
THEN A VOICE ANSWERS, "WHY? WHERE DO YOU WANT TO BE?"
SCHULZ

HOMEMADE VALENTINES
I NEED A VALENTINE THAT WILL IMPRESS THIS GIRL I LIKE..
FOR THE ♥ IN YOUR LIFE
THEN YOU'LL WANT THIS SUPER POTENT VALENTINE!
POTENT?
IT'LL SWEEP HER OFF HER FEET! IT'LL KNOCK HER SOCKS OFF!
ALL RIGHT, I'LL TAKE IT!
FOR THE ♥
GOOD.. IF YOU COME AROUND NEXT FRIDAY, YOU CAN PICK IT UP..
FRIDAY?! WHY CAN'T I HAVE IT NOW?
FOR THE ♥
IT'S TOO POTENT...
FOR THE ♥
THERE'S A FIVE-DAY WAITING PERIOD!
FOR THE ♥ IN YOUR LIFE
SCHULZ

I GUESS I LEAD KIND OF A SIMPLE LIFE..
BUT YOU KNOW WHAT I NEVER HAVE TO WORRY ABOUT?
LEAVING MY KEYS IN THE CAR..
SCHULZ

I'M GOING IN TO TOWN TO BUY VALENTINES FOR ALL THE GIRLS WHO LOVE ME..
I SHOULD BE BACK IN TEN SECONDS..
SCHULZ

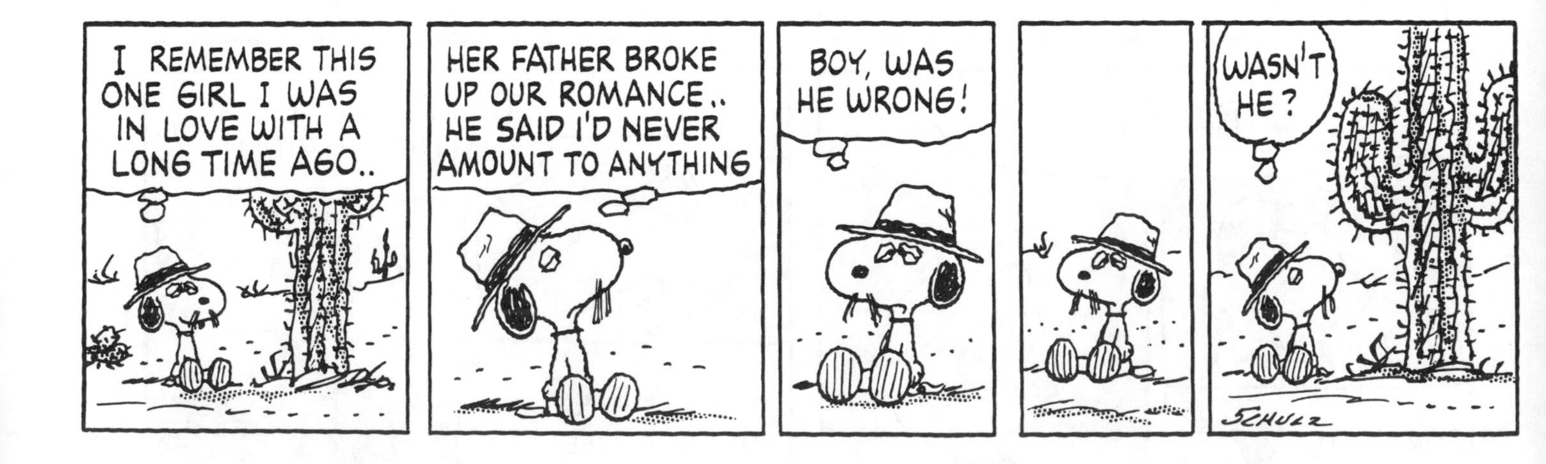
I REMEMBER THIS ONE GIRL I WAS IN LOVE WITH A LONG TIME AGO..
HER FATHER BROKE UP OUR ROMANCE.. HE SAID I'D NEVER AMOUNT TO ANYTHING
BOY, WAS HE WRONG!
WASN'T HE?
SCHULZ

LOOK, I GOT MYSELF A SLEEPING BAG..
I'M TIRED OF BEING COLD AT NIGHT
I WONDER WHO DESIGNS THESE THINGS..
SCHULZ

ROCK SLIDE AREA
SCHULZ

BIG BROTHER! WAKE UP! YOUR DOG IS IN THE HOSPITAL!
DAD TOOK HIM IN EARLY THIS MORNING!
YES, MA'AM, HIS NAME IS SNOOPY.. VISITORS? HE ALREADY HAS SOME VISITORS?
!
SCHULZ

I AM THE KING!
I AM THE KING OF THE HILL!
NO, YOU'RE NOT!
I AM THE KING OF THE HILL!
I AM THE KING OF THE HILL!
THE SMALLER THE KING, THE MORE THE TALK..
SCHULZ

ANDY! SPIKE! OLAF! HOW DID YOU KNOW YOUR BROTHER WAS SICK? HOW DID YOU FIND YOUR WAY HERE?
ANIMALS HAVE AN INSTINCT ABOUT THINGS LIKE THIS..
WE GO BY INSTINCT
A LOT OF IT WAS LUCK..
SCHULZ

OUR BROTHER SEEMS TO BE SLEEPING ALL RIGHT..
I'VE BEEN THINKING.. DO DOGS GO TO HEAVEN WHEN THEY DIE?
WHEN THEY WHAT?
WHEN THEY DIE..
I DIDN'T KNOW WE DIE!?
SCHULZ

WAITING ROOM
I HEARD A NURSE SAY OUR BROTHER SNOOPY HAS PNEUMONIA..
HE WAS ALWAYS THE LIVELY ONE IN OUR FAMILY..
WASN'T HE IN WORLD WAR I?
I THINK HE JUST THOUGHT HE WAS..
YOU KNOW WHAT I ALWAYS WONDERED?
WHERE DID HE GET THE HELMET AND GOGGLES?
SCHULZ

IF WE'RE ALL BROTHERS, HOW COME I'M SO FUZZY, YOU'RE SO SKINNY AND OLAF IS SO FAT?
I'M NOT SKINNY.. I'M TRIM!
AND I'M NOT FAT!
YOU'RE NOT FAT?
I'M ROLY-POLY!
SCHULZ

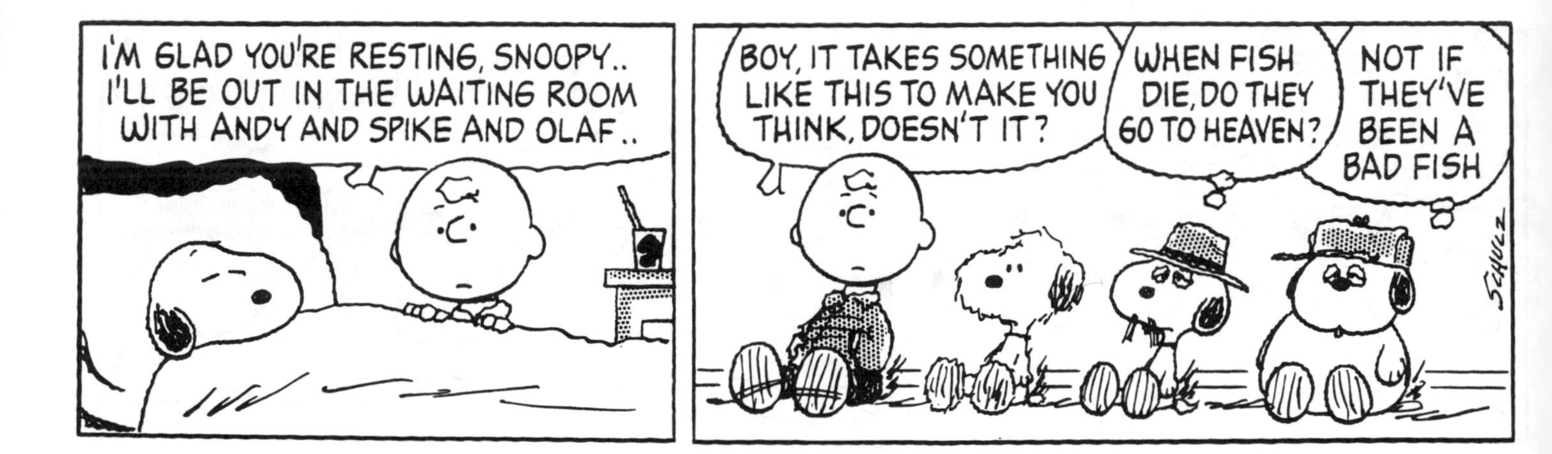
I'M GLAD YOU'RE RESTING, SNOOPY.. I'LL BE OUT IN THE WAITING ROOM WITH ANDY AND SPIKE AND OLAF..
BOY, IT TAKES SOMETHING LIKE THIS TO MAKE YOU THINK, DOESN'T IT?
WHEN FISH DIE, DO THEY GO TO HEAVEN?
NOT IF THEY'VE BEEN A BAD FISH
SCHULZ

HOW CAN WE KNOW IF OUR BROTHER IS GETTING BETTER IF NO ONE TELLS US ANYTHING?
I THINK I'LL GO HANG AROUND THE FRONT DESK.. MAYBE I'LL HEAR SOMETHING...
THE NURSE IS HAVING TROUBLE WITH HER BOYFRIEND, AND THE DOCTOR IS GOING TO SWITCH TO A METAL SEVEN-WOOD!
SCHULZ

YAWN
Z
SCHULZ

MOM? DAD? GUESS WHAT! SNOOPY IS AWAKE, AND HE'S EATING!
YES! HE'S REALLY ENJOYING HIS LUNCH ... IN FACT, THEY ALL ARE!
SCHULZ

I CAN'T BELIEVE IT.. YOUR BROTHERS HAVE GONE! THEY KNEW YOU WERE FEELING BETTER SO THEY JUST LEFT..
DOGS DON'T SAY, "GOODBYE"
SCHULZ

MY DOG IS HOME!
SCHULZ

WHEN YOUR DOG WAS SICK, YOU WERE WORRIED ABOUT HIM, WEREN'T YOU?
IF I GOT SICK, WOULD YOU WORRY THAT MUCH ABOUT ME?
OF COURSE
THAT MUCH, OR MORE?
I CAN'T HEAR YOU..THE TV IS TOO LOUD..
STUPID DOG!
SCHULZ

YOU'VE TIED YOUR OWN SHOES, RERUN! GOOD FOR YOU
NOW, OF COURSE, THERE'S ONE OTHER THING...
THE SOCKS GO ON BEFORE THE SHOES..

MARCIE, I DON'T UNDERSTAND THE PROBLEM ON PAGE 362..
THERE IS NO PROBLEM ON PAGE 362, SIR... THAT'S THE INDEX..
PRETTY TRICKY, MA'AM!
SCHULZ

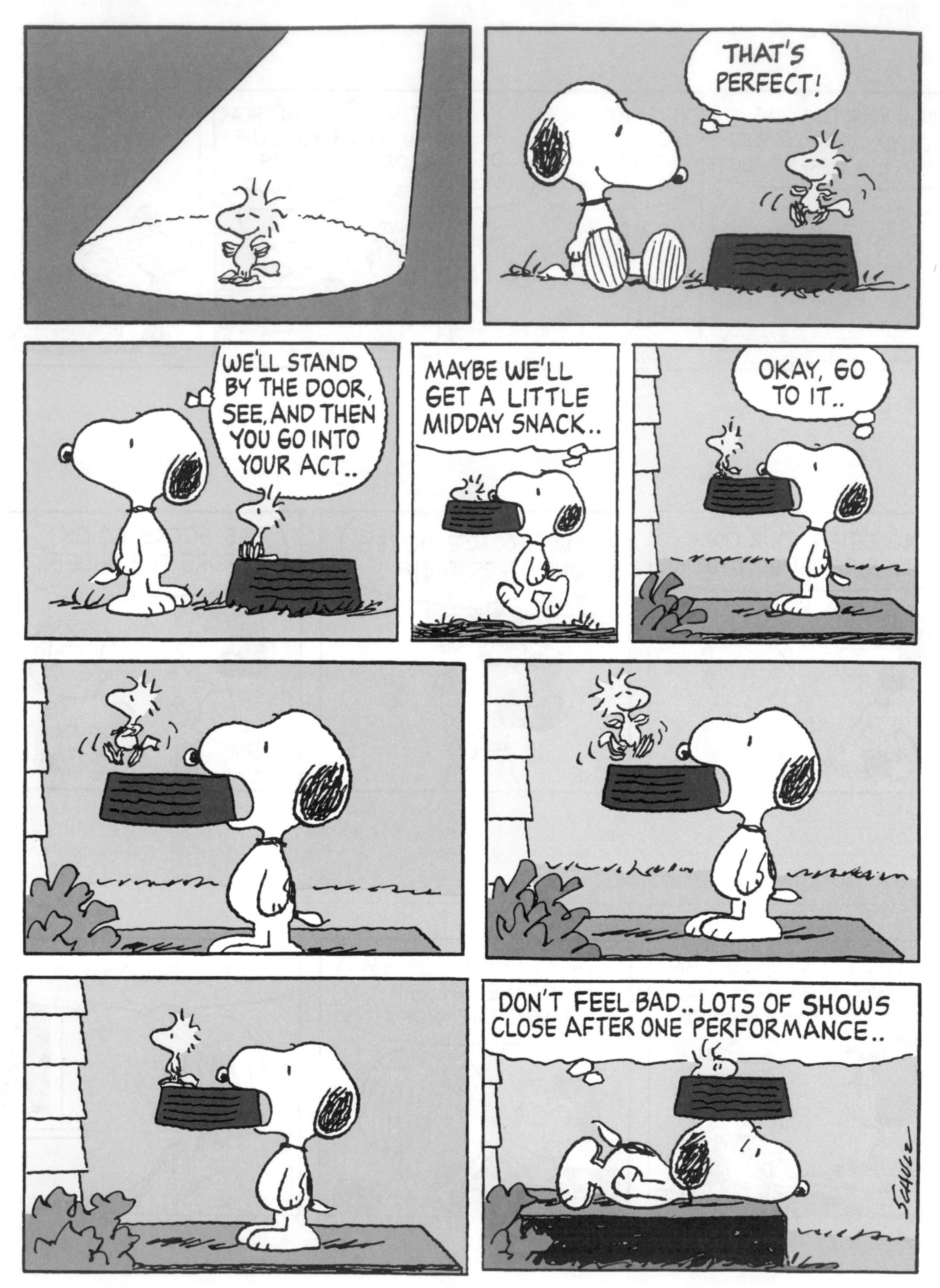
THAT'S PERFECT!
WE'LL STAND BY THE DOOR, SEE, AND THEN YOU GO INTO YOUR ACT..
MAYBE WE'LL GET A LITTLE MIDDAY SNACK..
OKAY, GO TO IT..
DON'T FEEL BAD.. LOTS OF SHOWS CLOSE AFTER ONE PERFORMANCE..
SCHULZ

TELL MY TEACHER TO BRING THE CLASS TO OUR HOUSE TODAY, AND WE CAN STUDY HERE IN MY ROOM..
SHE SAID IS IT ALL RIGHT TO BRING THE PRINCIPAL, TOO, AND ALL THE MEMBERS OF THE SCHOOL BOARD?
IT WOULD HAVE BEEN PRETTY CROWDED..
SCHULZ

WAKE UP! IT'S A PERFECT DAY FOR CHASING RABBITS!
WHAT ARE YOU DOING?
YOU DON'T CATCH RABBITS BY HANDING OUT LITERATURE..
SCHULZ

WAIT HERE.. I'LL GO SEE IF THERE ARE ANY COOKIES LEFT..
NOPE, THE COOKIES ARE ALL GONE..
SO I WASTED A GOOD COOKIE WAIT..
SCHULZ

THIS HAS BEEN A REALLY GOOD DAY..
I DID EVERYTHING RIGHT...
IN MY OPINION..
SCHULZ

"DOG FLAKES"? WHO ORDERED "DOG FLAKES"?!
SCHULZ

I LOVE THE START OF THE BASEBALL SEASON!
THERE'S A CERTAIN ALMOST INDESCRIBABLE FEELING IN THE AIR..
DEFEAT!
SCHULZ

Z
KLUNK!
SIR, WAKE UP.. YOU'RE IN THE WRONG DESK!
WAKE UP!!
KLUNK!
Z
SIR, WAKE UP BEFORE THE TEACHER COMES BACK!
KLUNK!
Dear Diary,
Strange day at school today. I started out feeling perky, and ended up in the wastebasket.
SCHULZ

HOW WOULD YOU LIKE TO BUY THE BAT THAT WAS USED BY ROY HOBBS?
ROY HOBBS WAS A FICTIONAL CHARACTER
SO IF I SOLD IT TO YOU, IT WOULD BE A REAL CON JOB..
THAT'S RIGHT..
I'LL TRY SOMEBODY ELSE...
HOW WOULD YOU LIKE TO BUY THE BAT THAT WAS USED BY ROY HOBBS?

LOOK WHAT I GOT! THAT WEIRD KID JUST SOLD ME THE BAT THAT WAS USED BY ROY HOBBS!
WHO WAS ROY HOBBS?
WHO WAS ROY HOBBS? ARE YOU KIDDING?
BOY, LOOK AT THIS BAT! THIS IS A REAL COLLECTOR'S ITEM!
WHO WAS ROY HOBBS?
I DON'T HAVE THE SLIGHTEST IDEA!

HI, CHARLIE BROWN..THIS IS THE WEIRD KID WHO SOLD ME THE BAT USED BY ROY HOBBS..
I ONLY PAID HER A DOLLAR, AND I GOT A REAL COLLECTOR'S ITEM
ROY HOBBS WAS A FICTIONAL CHARACTER
BE CAREFUL..YOU'RE MESSING UP MY PITCHER'S MOUND!

YOU SOLD ME A WORTHLESS BAT! I DID NOT! I WANT MY DOLLAR BACK! TRY AND GET IT! LET GO OF THAT BAT! LET GO YOURSELF! GIVE ME MY DOLLAR! LET GO! LET GO YOURSELF!!

CHARLIE BROWN, I WAS GOING TO ASK IF I COULD PLAY ON YOUR TEAM, BUT I'D NEVER WANT TO PLAY ON THE SAME TEAM WITH THIS STUPID GIRL!
OH, YEAH? I'M THE MOST FAITHFUL PLAYER HE HAS!
FAITHFUL TO WHAT?
THE CATCHER!
I CAN'T STAND IT!

IT'S ALMOST TIME FOR DINNER..
IF I MOVE, I'LL WAKE UP MY DOG..
PLEASE DON'T TALK..IT MAKES YOUR STOMACH GO UP AND DOWN, AND IT'S VERY DISTURBING

SLAM!
MOM SAYS NOT TO FLY YOUR KITE IN THE HOUSE..
SCHULZ

This is my report on dogs.
Dogs are good to have around because they are always alert.
Z
KLUNK!
Well, some of them are.
SCHULZ

SURPRISE! I DECORATED YOUR DINNER WITH A LITTLE FLAG!
IT LOOKS LIKE THE EIGHTH HOLE AT PEBBLE BEACH..
SCHULZ

POW!
HERE'S YOUR SOCK, CHARLIE BROWN..I COULDN'T GET THE BALL OUT..
SCHULZ

WELL, THAT'S IT, CHARLIE BROWN..WE LOST AGAIN
IN THE OLD DAYS, IF SOMEONE WAS DEFEATED, HE HELD UP A WHITE FLAG..
SCHULZ

Z
THE BALL WAS RIGHT OVER THE PLATE! WHY DIDN'T I SWING?!
Z
SCHULZ

I'M SORRY, MA'AM, IF MY TEST PAPER IS A LITTLE HARD TO READ...
I HAD TROUBLE WRITING IT BECAUSE THERE WAS SOMETHING ON MY DESK..
A HEAD!
Z
SCHULZ

MY PITCHER'S MOUND LOOKS GREAT..
IT'S GOING TO BE A GOOD SEASON, CHARLIE BROWN!
OUR OL' BACKSTOP SEEMS TO BE IN GOOD SHAPE..
HOW ABOUT THE OUTFIELD?
ALL MOWED, CHARLIE BROWN..IT'S BEAUTIFUL!
AND WE'VE RAKED THE INFIELD SO IT LOOKS BETTER THAN EVER..
THEN ALL WE HAVE TO WORRY ABOUT IS THE SOUND SYSTEM..
THE SOUND SYSTEM?
THIS YEAR LET'S TRY TO GET THE BALL OVER THE PLATE, YOU BLOCKHEAD!
THE SOUND SYSTEM IS STILL WORKING..
SCHULZ

HEY, CHUCK..I NEED YOUR HELP WITH A SCHOOL ASSIGNMENT
WE HAVE TO INTERVIEW A BUSINESSMAN..WHAT DOES YOUR DAD DO?
A BARBER? ASK HIM IF THAT'S A BUSINESS..
AN ART? WELL, I GUESS THAT'LL BE ALL RIGHT..
SCHULZ

YES, SIR, I'M SUPPOSED TO INTERVIEW A BUSINESSMAN SO I HAVE THESE QUESTIONS...
HOW DID YOU GET STARTED AS A BARBER?
IS THERE ROOM FOR ADVANCEMENT? WHAT ABOUT HEALTH CARE? IS IT A GOOD CAREER FOR WOMEN?
Y'ALL COME BACK NOW, Y'HEAR?
SCHULZ
YOU DID A NICE JOB ON THAT GUY..

THIS IS MY REPORT ON THE BUSINESSMAN BARBER I INTERVIEWED..
YEARS AGO, HE SAID, HAIRCUTS WERE THIRTY-FIVE CENTS AND ICE CREAM CONES WERE A NICKEL..
BRINGS BACK A LOT OF MEMORIES FOR YOU, HUH, MA'AM ?
SCHULZ

I THINK YOUR SHORTSTOP IS ASLEEP
IT'S THE DREAMING THAT GETS ME..
WOOF! WHIMPER.. WHINE... WHIMPER! WHIMPER!
SCHULZ

I'D HATE TO HAVE A JOB WHERE YOU HAD TO GET UP EARLY IN THE MORNING..
I'D HATE TO HAVE A JOB WHERE YOU STAYED IN THE SAME PLACE ALL DAY..
I'D HATE TO HAVE A JOB WHERE YOU HAD TO BE NICE TO EVERYBODY..
SCHULZ

THIS HAS BEEN A LONG UPHILL CLIMB..
BUT IT WAS WORTH IT, WASN'T IT?
OF COURSE, NOW WE HAVE THAT LITTLE PROBLEM OF GETTING DOWN..
SCHULZ

SO WHAT I'M SAYING HERE IS WE CAN'T COMPARE APPLES AND WATERMELONS..
OR GRAPES, OR PEARS, OR BANANAS, OR PEACHES, OR STRAWBERRIES, OR..
MA'AM?
ORANGES, SIR..
FORGET IT, MARCIE

HAS THE BUS COME YET?
IF THE BUS HAD COME, I'D BE ON IT, AND I'D BE HALF WAY TO SCHOOL BY NOW, AND I WOULDN'T BE HERE FOR YOU TO ASK ME!
CRABBY FLAKES FOR BREAKFAST AGAIN, HUH?

AND IT SAYS HERE THAT NO ONE HAS BEEN KNOWN TO HAVE BEEN STRUCK BY A FALLING METEORITE..
ALTHOUGH A DOG WAS KILLED IN EGYPT BY A METEORITE YEARS AGO..
WHAT DO THEY MEAN, "ALTHOUGH" A DOG?

HERE'S THE FIERCE JUNGLE ANIMAL SNEAKING UP ON HIS PREY...
USING ALL HIS NATIVE CUNNING, HE CREEPS UP BEHIND HIS VICTIM...
IS THIS THE FRONT OR THE BACK?

WHAT?
SORRY.. I CAN'T HEAR YOU WHEN THE WIND IS BLOWING!

PSYCHIATRIC HELP 5¢
SOME DAYS I'M UP, AND THE NEXT DAYS I'M DOWN
THE DOCTOR IS IN
LIKE AN EMOTIONAL ROLLER COASTER, HUH?
DO YOU EVER FEEL LIKE YOU'RE ON A ROLLER COASTER, CHARLIE BROWN?
THE DOCTOR IS IN
HOW ABOUT BUMPER CARS?

“ ”
, , , , , , ,
THESE ARE COMMAS.. IF A COMMA WORKS HARD, IT CAN BECOME AN APOSTROPHE, SEE?
The dog's bone. The cat's whiskers.
IF A COMMA FINDS A PARTNER, IT CAN GO INTO PAIRS..THEY CAN BECOME QUOTATION MARKS..
“Ah,” he said.
AREN'T THE ONES ON THE LEFT UPSIDE DOWN?
TO BECOME A REAL QUOTATION MARK, THEY HAVE TO LEARN TO DO A BACKFLIP..
I'D BETTER GO.. I HAVE SOME WRITING TO DO FOR HOMEWORK
WATCH THOSE QUOTATION MARKS WHEN THEY DO A BACKFLIP..
SCHULZ

I WONDER HOW THE COMPOSER COULD WRITE SOMETHING SO BEAUTIFUL..
I WONDER HOW THE VIOLINIST CAN REMEMBER ALL THOSE NOTES..
I WONDER HOW THEY CHANGE THOSE LIGHT BULBS WAY UP THERE IN THE CEILING..
SCHULZ

HI, CHARLES..WE'VE JUST BEEN TO A LONG SYMPHONY CONCERT
WHAT'S WRONG WITH PATTY?
SHE WAS MAHLERED!
SCHULZ

CHARLIE BROWN? I HAPPENED TO BE WALKING BY, AND I SAW THIS KITE ALL TANGLED UP IN THIS BIG BUSH, AND I WAS JUST WONDERING HOW..
DON'T ASK!
SCHULZ

SOME THINGS RUN IN THE FAMILY..
RATS!
SCHULZ

I SEE YOUR OPPONENT HAS TO GIVE YOU TWO STROKES ON EVERY HOLE... DOES THAT BOTHER YOU ?
JOE NO-PRIDE!
SCHULZ

NOW, AFTER WE TAKE FORT ZINDERNEUF, I HOPE A CERTAIN SOMEONE DOESN'T THINK WE'RE GOING TO HAVE A BIG PARTY..
SCHULZ

I LOVE MEETINGS ON THE MOUND!
ONE FINGER WILL MEAN A FAST BALL, AND TWO FINGERS A CURVE BALL..
TELL YOUR CATCHER I THINK HE'S CUTE..
SCHULZ
Did you tell him I think he's cute?

"WHAT'S THAT SUPPOSED TO MEAN?" THAT'S MY NEW PHILOSOPHY!
WHENEVER SOMEONE SAYS SOMETHING TO ME, I JUST SAY, "WHAT'S THAT SUPPOSED TO MEAN?"
I'M GLAD YOU TOLD ME.. NOW I WON'T SAY ANYTHING TO YOU
WHAT'S THAT SUPPOSED TO MEAN?
SCHULZ

GUESS WHAT..
YOU'RE A DOG, AND YOU'LL ALWAYS BE A DOG!
HOW REASSURING!
SCHULZ

DID BEETHOVEN EVER DO ANY ENDORSEMENTS? YOU KNOW, LIKE TENNIS SHOES OR SOMETHING?
NO! BEETHOVEN NEVER ENDORSED ANY TENNIS SHOES!!
KLUNK
THAT'S TOO BAD.. BEETHOVEN TENNIS SHOES WOULD HAVE GONE OVER BIG
SCHULZ

I MUST ADMIT, SIR, THAT I NEVER WOULD HAVE THOUGHT TO PUT A WATERMELON IN MY LUNCH..
SCHULZ

"HOWEVER, THE BIG PROBLEM IS AN OVERTURNED RIG AT THE CORNER OF THIRD AND MISSION"
SCHULZ
NO, THE BIG PROBLEM IS I HAVEN'T DONE ANY HOMEWORK..

OKAY, THERE'S FORT ZINDERNEUF! I NEED ONE VOLUNTEER TO GO AHEAD, AND DEMAND THEIR SURRENDER..
GOOD! IF THEY SURRENDER, THEY CAN HAVE A BALLOON
SCHULZ

OH, NO! LOOK WHO'S COMING..
THE DOCTOR IS IN
PSYCHIATRIC HELP 5¢
'PIGPEN,' YOU'RE A COMPLETE MESS!
THE DOCTOR IS IN
I WANT YOU TO GO HOME AND GET CLEANED UP..THEN WHEN YOU COME BACK, WE CAN HAVE A LITTLE TALK..
WOW! YOU LOOK GREAT! NOW WE CAN TALK ABOUT APPEARANCE, AND HOW IMPORTANT IT CAN BE...
THE DOCTOR
WE MAY NOT BELIEVE IT, BUT IT'S TRUE..
THE DOCTOR IS IN
WE MAY LIKE TO THINK APPEARANCE ISN'T..
THE DOCTOR IS IN
SIGH
THE DOCTOR IS IN
SCHULZ

YESTERDAY I STOOD HERE IN THE RAIN FOR TEN MINUTES WAITING FOR THE SCHOOL BUS..
AFTER I GOT TO SCHOOL, YOU KNOW WHAT I LEARNED? I LEARNED HOW WIDE THE MISSISSIPPI RIVER IS..
I STOOD IN THE RAIN FOR TEN MINUTES TO LEARN HOW WIDE THE MISSISSIPPI RIVER IS!
HOW WIDE **IS** THE MISSISSIPPI RIVER?
I FORGOT
SCHULZ

NEVER TRY TO KISS SOMEBODY THROUGH A CATCHER'S MASK!
SCHULZ

SHE CAUGHT IT!
REJOICE! "THOU SAWIST IT, AND DIDST REJOICE" I SAMUEL 19:5!
"AND THOU SHALT REJOICE IN EVERY GOOD THING" DEUTERONOMY 26:11
I HAVE A WEIRD TEAM..
SCHULZ

THROW IT, LUCY!
THROW THE BALL!
THROW IT! THROW IT! THROW IT!!
SORRY, MANAGER..IT TOOK ME A WHILE TO UNPLUG MY HAIR DRYER..

SOMETIMES I LIE AWAKE AT NIGHT, AND I ASK, "WHY AM I HERE? WHAT'S THE PURPOSE OF IT ALL? DOES MY LIFE HAVE ANY MEANING?"
THEN A VOICE COMES TO ME THAT SAYS, "FORGET IT! I HATE QUESTIONS LIKE THAT!"

CLICK!
I HAVE PHOTOS OF ALL MY SUPPER DISHES..
DO YOU WANT ONE FOR YOUR WALLET?

YOU HAVE A STRANGE GALLERY..
HERE'S THE WORLD FAMOUS GOLFER HITTING A BEAUTIFUL SHOT TO THE EIGHTEENTH GREEN..
HE MARKS HIS BALL WITH A CHOCOLATE-CHIP COOKIE..
THEN HE WALKS BACK TO GET HIS PUTTER..
NOW HE RETURNS TO THE GREEN TO SINK THE WINNING PUTT...
BUT THE BIRDS HAVE EATEN HIS BALL MARKER!
SCHULZ

I KNOW THE ANSWER!
I KNOW THE ANSWER!
THE ANSWER IS, AS WE ALL KNOW FROM PREVIOUS GENERATIONS, AND PERSONAL EXPERIENCE, AND CLIMATE CONDITIONS, AND DIAGRAMS, AND..
SIX!
YES, THE ANSWER IS SIX..
SCHULZ

OKAY, SAY, "BIRDSEED"
SCHULZ

AS SISTER AND BROTHER, YOU KNOW WHAT OUR PROBLEM IS? WE DON'T TRY HARD ENOUGH TO GET ALONG..
I MEAN, I TRY, BUT YOU DON'T..
SO EVERYTHING IS REALLY MY FAULT?
NOW, YOU'RE TRYING!
SCHULZ

I WONDER WHAT IT WOULD BE LIKE TO BE A DOG AND NOT HAVE TO DO ANYTHING..
MAYBE THEY THINK OF BARKING AS BEING WORK..
WOOF!
WHEW
THAT WAS EXHAUSTING!
SCHULZ

AS SISTER AND BROTHER, WE'RE ALMOST LIKE A TEAM..
I'M THE MANAGER, AND YOU'RE THE WORTHLESS PLAYER WHO IS GOOD FOR NOTHING EXCEPT SITTING ON THE BENCH!
IT'S GOING TO BE A LONG SEASON
SCHULZ

IF WE'RE A COUPLE OF FARM DOGS, OLAF, DON'T YOU THINK WE SHOULD BE DOING SOMETHING?
DON'T YOU THINK WE SHOULD BE USEFUL?
WE ARE USEFUL..
IF WE MOVE, THE BARN WILL FALL DOWN..
SCHULZ

Z
YAWN
YAWN
SCHULZ

CANOEING ALL THE WAY, HUH?
NO, THERE USED TO BE A CAMPGROUND DOWNSTREAM, BUT IT'S NOT THERE, ANYMORE
SCHULZ

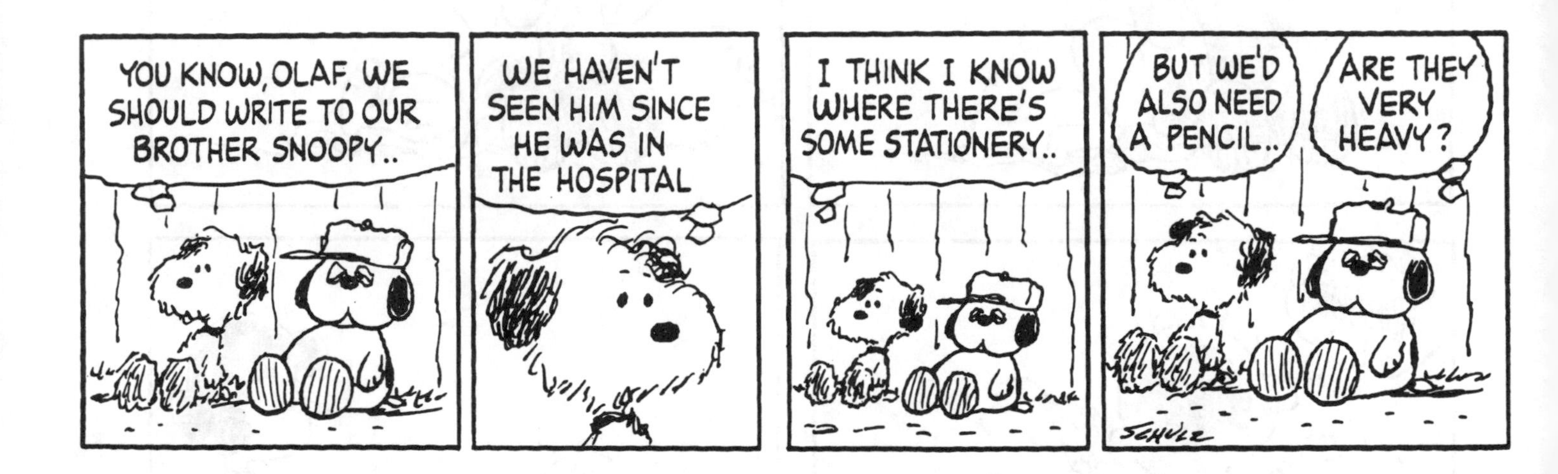
YOU KNOW, OLAF, WE SHOULD WRITE TO OUR BROTHER SNOOPY..
WE HAVEN'T SEEN HIM SINCE HE WAS IN THE HOSPITAL
I THINK I KNOW WHERE THERE'S SOME STATIONERY..
BUT WE'D ALSO NEED A PENCIL..
ARE THEY VERY HEAVY?
SCHULZ

ARE YOU PADDLING UPSTREAM OR DOWNSTREAM?
SORRY.. I DIDN'T MEAN TO CONFUSE YOU..
SCHULZ

I THINK SNOOPY WOULD ENJOY GETTING A LETTER FROM US
WE DON'T KNOW HOW TO WRITE, DO WE?
NO, REMEMBER WHAT I USED TO TELL YOU?
WHAT WAS THAT?
OBEDIENCE SCHOOL WAS A WASTE OF TIME!
SCHULZ

BE CAREFUL..
IF YOU PADDLE TO THE EDGE OF THE EARTH, YOU MIGHT FALL OFF..
SCHULZ

HEY, MANAGER.. ASK YOUR CATCHER IF HE'S GOING TO TAKE ME TO THE SENIOR PROM!
SHE WANTS TO KNOW IF YOU'RE GOING TO TAKE HER TO THE SENIOR PROM..
HE SAYS NOT IF YOU WERE THE LAST PERSON ON EARTH!
I'LL CANCEL THE LIMO..
SCHULZ

?
HA! I MADE YOU LOOK!
HEE HEE HEE
YOU THINK I'M SO DUMB I'D FALL FOR MY OWN TRICK?
I'M NOT GONNA LOOK..
SCHULZ

MOVE AWAY.. I'M TRYING TO GET A TAN
I'M NOT BOTHERING YOU
YOU'RE USING UP ALL THE SUN!

ALL RIGHT, TEAM, WE'RE ONLY ONE RUN BEHIND.. WE CAN WIN IF WE CONCENTRATE!
WE'RE CONCENTRATING!
WE'RE ALL CONCENTRATING..
Z
KLUNK!

I'M DESPERATELY IN NEED OF HELP WITH MY HOMEWORK..
ALL RIGHT, BUT YOU'RE GOING TO HAVE TO PAY ATTENTION..
NOW, IN THIS FIRST PROBLEM, THE..
I HATE PAYING ATTENTION..

HEY, PITCHER! YOU WANT SOME ADVICE?
WHAT KIND OF ADVICE COULD A PITCHER GET FROM AN OUTFIELDER?
YOU NEED A HAIRCUT!
SCHULZ

I HEAR YOU JUST LOST ANOTHER CASE..
IN THE OLD DAYS, WHEN AN ATTORNEY LOST A CASE, HE'D REND HIS GARMENTS..
NOWADAYS WE JUST KICK OUR HAT!
SCHULZ

From the day I was born my life has been hard.
THIS IS RIDICULOUS! YOU HAVE AN EASY LIFE!
Starting now, my life has been very hard.
SCHULZ

AAUGH!!
NOT AGAIN!
CAN'T YOU CATCH ANYTHING? HOW COULD YOU MISS IT?!
YOU'RE THE WORST PLAYER IN THE HISTORY OF THE GAME!
YOU'RE GOING TO DRIVE ME CRAZY!!
HOW CAN YOU BE SO BAD?!
ARE YOU TALKING TO ME?
SCHULZ

DON'T YOU THINK YOU SHOULD YELL "FORE!"?
DOGS CAN'T TALK..
BONK

One of my greatest thrills was being part of a dogsled team.
YOU WERE NEVER PART OF A DOGSLED TEAM..
Every winter the kid next door used to pull me on his sled.

THIS IS MY REPORT ON HAMLET..
A HAMLET IS A SMALL VILLAGE WITH A POPULATION OF MAYBE A FEW HUNDRED, AND..
MA'AM?
FAR AND AWAY, SIR, ONE OF THE GREAT TRIES OF ALL TIME!
I CAN'T STAND IT..

SIT ON THE BALL, MARCIE, AND I'LL TAKE YOUR PICTURE
WHY DON'T I DO A SLAM-DUNK?
YOU COULDN'T SLAM-DUNK A DOUGHNUT! JUST SIT ON THE BALL!
MAYBE YOU'RE RIGHT, MARCIE.. HOW ABOUT A SLAM-KLUNK?
SCHULZ

I JUST CAN'T BELIEVE HOW STUPID YOUR STORIES ARE!
IN FACT, I CAN'T SEE ANYTHING GOOD AT ALL ABOUT YOUR WRITING!
I HAVE NEAT MARGINS..

SMALLEST DESERT I'VE EVER SEEN..

WELL, DID YOU ENJOY THE BOOK ?
I DON'T KNOW.. I SLEPT ALL THE WAY THROUGH IT..
SCHULZ

I NEED HELP WITH MY HOMEWORK
AGAIN?
YOU KNOW, I'M NOT ALWAYS GOING TO BE AROUND TO HELP YOU..
HOW OLD DO YOU THINK YOU'RE GOING TO BE BEFORE YOU WON'T NEED ME ANYMORE?
EIGHTY !
SCHULZ

DO YOU HAVE ANY REGRETS, CHARLIE BROWN?
LOTS OF THEM..
I REGRET THE BITES I SHOULD HAVE BITTEN..
SCHULZ

LOOK AT THIS, MARCIE! SHE GAVE ME A FAILING GRADE ON MY THEME!
I'M TOTALLY CRUSHED! I WAS SURE I WAS GOING TO GET A GOOD GRADE!
THIS IS A BLANK SHEET OF PAPER..
BUT THE POTENTIAL WAS THERE!!
SCHULZ

I HAVE SOMETHING TO SAY TO YOU THAT WILL MAKE YOUR HAIR STAND ON END..
I SAID IT WILL MAKE YOUR HAIR STAND ON END!
THAT'S BETTER..
SCHULZ

LET ME EXPLAIN..
THE DOCTOR IS IN
PSYCHIATRIC HELP 5¢
IT'S A RELAXING TECHNIQUE
THE DOCTOR IS IN
I WANT YOU TO PICTURE YOURSELF STANDING IN A BEAUTIFUL MEADOW
IMAGINE THE SOFT RAYS OF THE SUN PENETRATING YOUR WHOLE BODY..
THEN TRY TO IMAGINE THE MOST WONDERFUL GENTLE BREEZE CARESSING YOUR UPTURNED FACE..
CAN YOU DO THAT, CHARLIE BROWN?
THE DOCTOR IS IN
YOU'RE STANDING OUT IN THIS BEAUTIFUL MEADOW..WHAT ARE YOU THINKING?
IT'S ONLY THE FIRST INNING, AND THE OTHER TEAM HAS ALREADY SCORED FORTY RUNS!
THE DOCTOR
SCHULZ